MIRACLES, MYSTERIES, MEMOIRS

A Collection of True Stories

Sushila Rani Mathur

ARTHUR H. STOCKWELL LTD
Torrs Park   Ilfracombe   Devon
Established 1898
www.ahstockwell.co.uk

© *Sushila Rani Mathur, 2009*
First published in Great Britain, 2009
All rights reserved.
No part of this publication may be reproduced
or transmitted in any form or by any means,
electronic or mechanical, including photocopy,
recording, or any information storage and
retrieval system, without permission
in writing from the copyright holder.

British Library Cataloguing-in-Publication Data.
A catalogue record for this book is available
from the British Library.

Arthur H. Stockwell Ltd bears no responsibility
for the accuracy of events recorded in this book.

IN MEMORY OF MY PARENTS
Mr Brij Govind Mathur
and
Mrs Bishan Pyari Mathur
and
My Husband, Professor P. N. Mathur
and
My Son, Rajul P. Mathur

DEDICATED TO

The Lotus Feet
of
The Divine Mother

ISBN 978-0-7223-3903-9
Printed in Great Britain by
Arthur H. Stockwell Ltd
Torrs Park   Ilfracombe
Devon

CONTENTS

Foreword	5
Acknowledgements	6
Preface	8
Help from the Heavens	11
The Kite or the Big Eagle	16
The Never-Ending Five Miles	21
In Between a Tiger and a Tigress	33
The Sugar-Eater	62
The Picture	78
Diamonds Are Not for Ever	83
The Power of Prayer, or a Miracle	94
The Adventures of My Very First Trip to America	102
The Washerman and the Panther	115
The Deadly Snakes in our Garden	121
A Sunday Soon after My Father's Retirement	130
The Divine Bough	138
You Would Not Believe It	147

FOREWORD

Life is multidimensional. Certain incidents suddenly make a deep impression on our minds. Full of excitement and enthusiasm we try to record them at our leisure. These incidents surely become, 'emotion recollected in tranquillity', as Wordsworth puts it.

The following true stories present some of such unbelievable, unforgettable, personal experiences of my dear sister, Sushila Rani Mathur, who migrated to England in the later half of the previous century.

I have great pleasure in offering them to our brilliant readers in their original form. The writer's extraordinary sensibility and sensitivity to ordinary events is remarkable. Her style is as natural and unsophisticated as her vivid descriptions of nature.

Rama Rani Lal, November 2006.

ACKNOWLEDGEMENTS

It is by the grace of God, blessings from my elders and help from my children that I have been able to jot down some of the very extraordinary experiences and incidents of my life. God gave me the inspiration, my children gave me the encouragement and my brothers and sisters provided me with the details that I had forgotten in some of the incidents. I am sincerely and deeply grateful to them all for their help in one way or another.

I used to send away the first drafts of my stories to my brothers, Mr Mahesh Govind and Mr Omesh Govind, for their approval to make sure that what I had written was correct. Then about six years back my sister, Mrs Urmila Rani, came to Britain to be with me for a few days. She did a great job. She sorted out all my complete papers from the pile of incomplete and other rough works, put them in order and made a list of all the stories I had written till that time and took them with her to India to show to her husband, who is a retired professor of English in Ajmer, India. This was the very first step in the shaping of this book. I am very thankful to her and also to my brothers for their kind help and encouragement.

My special thanks go to my younger sister, Mrs Rama Rani Lall, who is a professor of English at Maharani College Jaipur. (She is officially retired now but has been requested to continue taking some classes still.) It is she who collected all my stories from my brothers and sisters and not only read them with great interest, but also compiled them in one place, got photocopies made of all the articles she had with her at that time, wrote a foreword and got them bound in spiral binders so that they were all at one place and could be given to anyone who might be interested in reading them. It is she who gave the name and shape to my writings. I am sincerely very grateful to her for all the effort and initiative she has taken in shaping this book.

My greatest and deepest thanks go to my son-in-law, Mr. Guy Footring, and my daughter Mrs.Shri Nidhi Footring. They both not only very lovingly but also very laboriously went through each page of each story as I wrote it and pointed out all the slips and mistakes that I had made in typing and writing. I am very, very grateful to them both for the suggestions and corrections they had to make in the very first drafts of each story. Without their continuous help and support this work would not have been possible at all. Their help was not only invaluable in the initial stages but also in the final stages of putting the book on a disk and sending it to the publishers.

Then their help in proof reading and typing out the errata and sending the final version again to the publishers – the credit for all these also goes to them.

I am also very thankful to them for keeping my computer going, with which I get stuck quite often. Buying and changing ink cartridges in my printer is beyond me, similarly, for all the rest of the small and big problems that they had to sort out for me. I am very grateful to them both for doing all these extra jobs as well for me.

Last, but not least, many thanks to my youngest grandchildren, dear Varun and Vikram Footring, who always listened to my stories with great interest and have written a few words about their grandma to go on the back cover of the book.

I would also like to thank The Directors of Stockwell Publishing Co. for keeping an active interest in getting my book published and providing the black-and-white sketches for most of my stories.

My many thanks to all my readers who have taken the trouble of getting this book and reading these stories. I hope they will enjoy reading them.

PREFACE

In the modern times of nuclear families, children often miss out on the company and experience of elders of the family. Many parents feel that not only grandchildren but even their own children hardly come to know much about the past of their families and their background. This is how I feel for my family at least. When the children used to be with us during their schooldays they did not have much time to spend with us, because we had migrated from India to Britain where the education system and standards were different from their schools in India, and they really had to work very hard to get used to the British system of education and catch up with the curriculum in their respective classes. Not only the children but even I had to work very hard in running the house without any household help, to which I was not at all used to. I used to get totally exhausted by evening and hardly had any energy left to talk or spend time chatting with the family.

The only time we all sat together and talked was the dinner times at night. My husband generally dominated the conversation because I used to be busy with making and serving hot chappatis to the family – a chore which I enjoyed very much. The general conversation topics at the table were either politics (in which I had the least interest and in which no one in my family took any active part) or my husband's non-professional papers on astronomy, history (mainly ancient history), archaeology and astronomy, about which all my children were quite enthusiastic. My younger son, Rajul, had a keen interest in astronomy from his very early childhood. When he was only fourteen and a half years old he had requested his father, who was going to Japan for one of his International conferences, to bring him a telescope from there. My husband brought one of the very best telescopes for him with a 4" reflector. This turned out to be the biggest and the most powerful telescope in the whole of Pune.

With this telescope Rajul had measured the movement of the Sun during a Solar Eclipse and took photographs of it at regular intervals. This photograph of his became one of the best photographs of the Solar Eclipse of that year and was published in many Astronomical journals.

One of the most renowned astronomers of India, Professor Bhalerao of Nasik, dedicated his book on Astronomy to my son Rajul when he was hardly fifteen and a half years old.

In some of my extraordinary encounters and adventures the children themselves were present at the scene, so what to tell them about them? Moreover, at that time there were more urgent things to attend to than to think over the incident. There would be talk about it for a day or two, then forgotten. The present is always so demanding that there is hardly any time left to reflect on the past. At that time our extraordinary experiences did not even strike us as being anything very much out of the ordinary. They were just part of our day-to-day life, so what was there to talk about them? It was only when we happened to meet our extended families and told them about our adventures that we realised they were not just ordinary incidents but real miracles or mysteries, which may seem very hard to believe, but then sometimes "facts are stranger than fiction". It was not only the children of those households but also the adults of the family who would listen to them with great interest and enthusiasm – especially our Agra family people.

Outside India one such great enthusiast is my nephew, Mr Ashish Mathur of Canada. Whenever I happened to visit my brother in Canada my little nephew would come to me and ask me to narrate my experiences, which he called my 'stories', but my brother and sister-in-law often thought more about me than him. They thought that he was unnecessarily bothering me, so quite often he was told off "Can't you see Bhuaji is busy?" or "We are talking to Bhuaji at the moment – you come later" or "Bhuaji is tired – let her rest." When it happened two or three times I could see the disappointment in my nephew's face. So one day I told him, "Don't worry I shall write them down for you."

"Yes Bhuaji, please do."

That is how it all started. It was on the insistence of my nephew that I wrote my very first article in English. I had written one or two before in my mother tongue, Hindi, but since my nephew was brought up in Canada, he hardly knew any Hindi. He does understand a bit of the spoken language but written Hindi is out of question. He could not read it then and cannot read it even now. So for his sake I made my very first attempt to write in English. As a matter of fact, the very first article that I wrote, 'Help from the Heavens', I dedicated to him because it was due to him that I wrote it, as that was the latest incident of that time.

Once started, I enjoyed writing more. Now some of them are here for you. They are all accounts of absolutely true incidents that had happened in my life. Since I am writing for the family I have not changed any names of persons or places, lest they lead to confusion. There is only one exception. Perhaps you will be able to guess it correctly yourself. I do sincerely hope that you will enjoy reading these extraordinary experiences of my life as much as those who have already read or listened to our adventure stories before from me first-hand.

HELP FROM THE HEAVENS

It was summer 1974. I was struggling to learn driving at the mature age of forty-seven. My older children, the two boys, had already been driving for some years and were quite expert drivers, so every now and then I used to go practising with them. I was still too scared to go into the busy roads of our town or on the winding, narrow roads through the undulating hills of the Welsh countryside around Aberystwyth, where we lived. Instead, I preferred to go to the family's favourite picnic spot, Ynyslas Beach, some twelve miles away from our home in Aberystwyth, a small picturesque seaside town in Wales. Ynyslas Beach is a vast sandy area of unique natural beauty, between the attractive sand dunes covered with tall wild grasses on one side and the town of Aberdovey on the other. The River Dovey and another, smaller, river flow gently between the vast sand dunes and the town of Dovey, the two merging their waters with the majestic sea beyond. The vast, sandy, sloppy beach stretches from the sand dunes to the shores of the sea and the rivers, covering a huge area, about a mile long and half a mile broad.

That day I had requested my younger son, Rajul, to take me to this beautiful, lovely, lonely beach. My youngest daughter, Shri Nidhi, about eight years old at that time, came along with us to play on the beach, which is quite a popular place with the local residents as well as tourists from all over Britain. Normally even on quiet days, there were usually at least a few cars parked by the sand dunes and a few people around, but that day there was absolutely no one in sight anywhere: no cars, no scooters, no vans, no caravans – not even a trace of anything. Let alone cars and people, not even seagulls were visible on that Wednesday afternoon. There was absolutely no living thing in sight. In my mind I thought, "Good! I have the whole beach to myself today, and I can practise as much as I like. I can run the car across diagonally, make circles on the sand, try sharp turns or master my steering by just zigzagging all the way across the huge, empty expanse of shiny sand."

The sea seemed far, far off. The tide was the lowest we had ever seen there before. The sea was unusually calm, as if the waves were having a leisurely time relaxing in the midday sun. Even the big River Dovey, which runs to meet the sea at this place, seemed nothing more than a shiny silvery streak on that bright summer afternoon.

My son parked the car at a safe distance from the water's edge but towards the spot where the two rivers meet the sea. The three of us got out of our car all excited. My daughter ran towards where the two rivers converge with the sea and played in the water. She made sandcastles in the sand, built domes over her feet, and collected shells and pebbles. My son played Frisbee with his sister for some time and then got busy taking photographs of the beautiful natural scenery all around.

All of us were having a great time and great fun. I thought I would practise my driving after the children finished playing, making sandcastles and collecting shells, etc. I was quietly admiring the serene beauty of the place and watching the children play happily around.

Suddenly my daughter shouted, "Mummy, where has my castle gone?"

I looked to where the castle was, and realised that the tide had started rising, and her sandcastle had already gone under the water. Several times before we had seen the tide rising. Actually it was one of my family's favourite pastimes to dig lines on the sand, one after another, or to place some markers and delightfully watch the waves rising inch by inch as they reached from one line to the next. It used to take about ten to fifteen minutes for the water to reach from one line to the other one above.

Accordingly we used to move our car backwards further up and up, away from the waves.

That day, however, the water seemed to be rising much faster than we had ever seen before. Our car, which was a good twenty-five to thirty feet away from the shore, was soon at the water's edge. My son quickly tried to move it back as usual, but that day, as soon as he tried to reverse, the wheels got stuck in the wet sand. The harder he tried, the deeper the wheels went. We tried with all our might to push the car back with our hands, but the car would not budge. Soon the water was touching the tyres and was rising rapidly. The place where we had been playing just a while ago was all underwater.

I told my son to run up to the hill where there was an emergency telephone and call for help. We all started running fast towards the dunes, but the water was rushing faster behind us. We looked around desperately for help, but there was absolutely no one in sight all around. It seemed certain that by the time my son would reach the top of the hillock, where the telephone was, the water would be on top of our car. I literally had to drag my little daughter, holding her hand, and ran as fast as I could to save our lives from the raging waters behind us. It was heartbreaking to leave the car behind and see it drowning helplessly in the merciless sea, but there was no other choice. With a very heavy heart we had to leave our car to its fate and try to save our own lives.

The waves were gushing in with frightening speed now. I wondered how I was ever going to tell my husband, who was in India at that time, that we had drowned his little white beauty, our almost new, beautiful Austin. The thought was gnawing at my heart. Suddenly I felt an irresistible urge to have a last look at our beautiful car, now drowning helplessly under the raging waves.

But lo and behold! What did I see? I could not believe my eyes. My eyes remained wide open as I beheld two giant men – quite dark in colour and heavily built. They looked at our car and then looked at me and asked smilingly, "You want this car out?"

Bewildered and astonished, in awe I looked at them and managed to mutter, "Yes please."

Right in front of my eyes, the two men lifted up the car, one holding it at the back and the other at the front. They carried it in their hands as if it was just a toy and put it several hundred feet further up the beach on the high and dry ground by the sand dunes. As they carried it, I walked fast on their left side.

Once they put the car down I quickly came forward to say my heartfelt thanks to them, but – wonder of wonders! – where were they? There was absolutely no trace of them: no footprints, no sound, no sign – nothing at all. We looked all around with wide-open eyes as far as the eyes could see, but there was no one at all – no sight or sound or soul anywhere at all. There was no ripple on the waves, no flutter in the skies, no footprints on the sands! Where had they gone? Where had they evaporated? They had simply melted away as suddenly and miraculously as they had materialised. My thanks hung in the air.

To this day, in the millennium year, I am as much bewildered and puzzled as I was on that eventful day. Who were they? Where had they come from? Where had they gone? Who had sent them? From where had they been keeping an eye on us? And, most amazing of all, how and where had they evaporated? These are the questions which have been puzzling me ever since, but I have found no answers yet.

I think that it will remain a mystery to me and to my children as long as we live. Certainly they were not people from Wales, or from England – no, not even from this our planet earth. Who were they then? So dark, so strange and so big! All that I can think of is that they were "Help from the Heavens".

THE KITE OR THE BIG EAGLE

"Finish your milk and take a fruit; take a banana or an orange and then only go out to play," I said with the authority of an elder sister over her younger sisters.

I used to try to persuade my sweet little sisters, Rama and Veena, who were as good friends to each other as sisters to eat something before they went out to play. It was their habit that, as soon as they would come home from their school, they would dump their school bags in one corner of their room and rush out to the front garden of our big bungalow. There they would play and sing or enjoy themselves plucking and eating the sweet, little red berries which grew in abundance on the hills and dales around our big bungalow. In fact, the garden after a certain point was nothing more than a huge rockery full of unkempt wild shrubs that grew on the slopes of the stony rugged valley lying in front of our bungalow.

We children were quite small when, most unfortunately, we had lost our mother. I was just about twelve years old and my youngest sister Veena was hardly eight months old at that time. After her death, our father, who was a real *karmyogi* in the true sense of the word, brought us up with extreme love and care. My *naniji* doted on us all. My mother, being the eldest of her family had a special place in my maternal grandparents' house. My *nanaji* and *naniji* had both pleaded hard with my father to leave us, their grandchildren with them because they thought that they would be able to look after us better than our father alone could after the sad demise of our mother. My uncles and aunts and all others in the family had tried their best to persuade our father to leave us in their care, but my father listened to none. He kept all his children with him all the time and showered all the love of a mother as well as of a father on us all.

After the marriages of my elder sisters, I was the eldest child in the family at that time and thought it my responsibility to look after my younger brother, Omesh, and sisters Kinni and Veena. In that capacity I would ask them to have something to eat before going out to play or sing or do whatever they wanted. But on this occasion my fairylike little sisters had ideas of their own and, ignoring my words, they rushed out saying, "Jiji, the berries in the garden are far more tasty than bananas or apples on the table."

They ran out, with their dupattas fluttering in the air like beautiful butterflies, and soon they were lost amidst the shrubs and bushes of the valley that spread out in front of our bungalow. Our bungalow was built in the middle section of a hill. In the front, after the green oval lawn and the broad driveway all around it, was the valley. A thick hedge of silky leaves of waist-high plants, in front and to the side of the oval even ground, separated the bungalow from the rugged valley down below. The rest of the hill was at the back of the bungalow but all within the high boundary wall around the bungalow.

My sisters wound their way down into the rugged valley, chatting, singing and moving from bush to bush, picking and eating the very tasty, sweet and sour, small red bush berries (*jhar beri*). By the way, they were both very good, natural talented singers with very sweet voices. I enjoyed watching them and listening to their sweet Rajasthani songs, which they had picked up in their school.

I was studying for my Bachelor of Arts examinations in those days. My sisters were in sixth and seventh classes in the high school. To watch over my sisters I used to take a book and sit on one of the easy chairs, which were kept in the large, long veranda in front of the bungalow outside the sitting room and my father's bedroom.

I liked sitting there in the evenings, not only to keep an eye on my sisters but also to admire the natural breathtaking beauty of the setting sun behind the deep-green curtain of tall, lush trees, which grew on the solitary, beautiful island in the midst of the beautiful blue Fateh Sagar Lake and the hills beyond. The gentle crimson rays of the sun brightened up the distant blue sky, and the wavy shadows danced in the beautiful blue lake below, creating a scene which was out of this world – especially if the bright evening star, Venus, with its golden glory was also following the silently setting sun. The blue sky above and the shimmering lake below, with the golden sun between the two, and the green thickets on the hills, presented an absolutely magical picture from our bungalow.

On that particular evening, I was engrossed in admiring the scenery with my book in front of me, when suddenly I saw a huge kite or a big eagle dive down exactly where my sisters were. They shrieked aloud with sheer fear.

I threw my book aside and got up with a jerk to make sure that they were not hurt by the big kite.

I was about to shout to the servants for help, but lo and behold! what did I see? It was absolutely unbelievable! I saw the big kite flying off clutching a very long, big snake tightly in its beak! The hood of the deadly silvery-black serpent was hardly two inches above my little sister's head and the tail was almost touching my other sister's side. I gasped with fright, hoping that the snake had not bitten them.

By that time the servants too had come rushing down. They had heard the loud shriek of my sisters. They too were dumbfounded at the sight they beheld. None of them had ever seen such a sight before.

My father had not yet returned from his office, but I rushed down to see that my sisters were all right. They were in a sort of state of shock at the kite diving right in front of them. Totally absorbed in singing and chatting and eating they had not noticed the snake lurking right at their feet on the ground. It was the sudden dive of the kite that had frightened them, not the snake (which, fortunately or unfortunately, they had not seen). It was only after the kite had flown to some height away from them that they noticed the snake in the kite's beak. By that time we were all with them on the spot watching the kite soaring higher and higher up in the sky with the big serpent dangling from its beak. It flew past the boundary wall of our bungalow, across the road, over the Lake View bungalow of the Singhal family, high up in the sky, out of sight somewhere over the lake.

The sight of the kite soaring high in the sky with the snake in its bite was so thrilling and unimaginable a thing that we almost forgot to ask our sisters how they were. It was only when the kite with its precious poisonous catch was out of sight that we turned our attention to dear Kinni and Veena.

"Are you OK?" with great concern I had inquired. "Are you feeling all right?"

Still shivering from shock, they replied, in quivering voices, "Yes! We are OK."

"How was it that you did not see such a big snake sneaking right at your feet?"

They really had no reasonable answer to this question except that they were too busy enjoying the berries.

"Did you feel any bite from the snake?"

"No, we did not feel anything."

Hearing this, I gave a sigh of relief that at least there was no danger of snake poison in their bodies. By the grace of God, they had been saved from the snakebite by the timely intervention of divine help in the form of the kite. Had they taken another step forward, the deadly snake might have bitten any of them. Thank God they were saved and safe!

I firmly believe now that we may not be able to see God, but He never fails to keep an eye on us. This belief has not only stayed with me all my life but has grown from strong to stronger with each passing year.

THE NEVER-ENDING FIVE MILES

It was the summer of the year 1942. My sister, Shanti Jiji, and I had just finished our high school. Our older sister, Radhe Jiji, had finished her BA finals. Our brother, Mahesh Dada, had finished his Faculty of Arts exams and, most importantly, our youngest maternal uncle, Mr H. B. Mathur, who later became a very famous physician, had very successfully got through his second year of medical school in spite of his serious illness with typhoid and pleurisy. The elders of the family were very keen that he should be sent to a hill station to recuperate his health, so my father, Mr B. G. Mathur, invited him to Simla, where he had got himself transferred from Delhi after my mother's very untimely death. We used to stay in Simla permanently, winter and summer.

We were thoroughly enjoying our first summer vacation in Simla in the great company of our youngest uncle, who was only just about a few months older than my elder sister, Radhe Jiji. We were all in a great holiday mood, having finished our finals of that year. The Simla climate is very pleasant in the months of June and July, so we used to go out for picnics and outings practically every day, especially to entertain our uncle and also so that he could get as much fresh air and sunshine as possible.

One fine day it occurred to us that why don't we go somewhere further and more exciting than just the nearby Glen and Chadwick

Falls or even the high up Jaku Temple on top of a nearby hill, or the coffee houses on the mall. We discussed the matter with our eldest first cousin (my father's elder brother's son), Babu Dada, who used to stay with us with his wife. He was a permanent resident of Simla from a much earlier time than us. He suggested that if we really wanted to go somewhere more exiting and more beautiful, then we could go to see the source of the great River Satluj, which, according to his knowledge and estimate was just about five miles away from our home. That sounded really exiting, so that evening as soon as our father returned from his office, we children surrounded him and put forward our proposal. He thought for a while because he was not so sure if the place was really accessible or whether we would be able to walk that far, but knowing my uncle's love of excursions, and having confidence in him, he gave his permission. He told us that we, the older children, could go but it would be too much for the younger ones. Fortunately I was included in the older children, maybe because I studied in the same class as my elder sister, Shanti Jiji, and we were always counted together for everything. My younger brother, Omesh and my two younger sisters, Kinni and Veena, were to stay behind with our *bhabiji*, Babu Dada's wife, who was not much interested in climbing up and down the hills with us lot.

My father called the servants and ordered them to get ready all the picnic things that we would need for our long excursion. Lots of fruits and snacks and other delicacies like cakes and pastries, and of course the standard picnic lunch of puri and aloo, were to be prepared. The sturdier of the two kitchen servants, who were local people of Simla, was assigned to accompany us. All that stuff needed some preparation, so it was decided that we should go the day after next, which I think was a Thursday. It was definitely a working day because I remember for sure that father as well as our cousin, Babu Dada, had to go to their offices and our younger brother and sisters had to go to their schools.

By the way, Simla used to be the summer capital of the British rule, and the schools and colleges used to have long vacations in winter, not in summer.

When our father moved to Simla after our mother's untimely death, we, the elder children, who were in our final years of studies, had to be left behind in Delhi with our uncles and aunts to finish our final exams. Thus it was exiting for us to go to Simla for the very first time that summer. Now that our Uncle Chote Mama had also joined us, we were in a great mood for outings and picnics. Our father had started calling us *sailanies*, which literally means 'the wanderers' or 'the sightseers'.

That Thursday morning, with all preparations in readiness, we (i.e. Chote Mama, Radhe Jiji, Mahesh Dada, Shanti Jiji, myself and our servant carrying all our picnic stuff) started early from home at about 5.30 a.m. We had to return back definitely by 6 p.m., according to our fathers instructions, and we wanted to spend as much time as possible by the riverside. In about an hour we reached Chota Simla, a suburb which was about three miles away from the main capital, Simla. We were supposed to stop there for breakfast, but we were all in such high spirits that nobody wanted to stop. We wanted to spend the maximum time at the riverbank, so we marched on in the good hope of reaching the river soon. According to our estimate, it was now just about only two miles away.

We walked another three miles or so, but there was no trace of any river anywhere, so we asked a chance passer-by how far the origin of the River Satluj was.

He replied matter-of-factly, "Oh, it is just about five miles."

How could that be? We thought we had already walked more than five miles. Anyway, we decided to rest for a little while and have some fruits, etc.

Having rested a while, we started back on our track. There was a winding narrow path going all along the edge of the mountains. To our surprise, after Chota Simla the hills were not so densely covered with tall pine trees as most of the others hills around. Pine trees were there but scattered here and there. As we proceeded, the footpath got a bit wider and the trees grew more sparsely. The hills were mostly barren except for low-growing grass. By now the sun had started rising from behind the yonder hills and we were enjoying the glory of the morning sun spreading its crimson rays over the lofty Himalayan Mountains.

Suddenly I felt as if a scorpion had stung me. I looked around for the scorpion but there was none to be seen.

Our local guide, our servant, said, "Don't walk so close to the mountain. It is full of the *bicchu buti*." *Bicchu buti* is something like poison ivy or stinging nettles in the Western world. In my excitement I had not paid much attention to the low-growing bicchu buti plants, which spread right across the footpath. It was the broad leaves of the bicchu buti that had brushed against my ankles and lower feet and caused the pain – not the sting of a scorpion.

To the wonder of us all, the next hill had another surprise for us. Instead of the green grass and brown mud, the soil was black, not only on the footpath but all the way down the hill. It looked like an old open coal mine. The coal apparently had been dug out long ago, but the soil was still black and soft to walk on. Fortunately we saw a few people also around. Our hopes were aroused that we were nearing our destination.

Still, to make sure, we asked them: "How far is the source of the River Satluj from here?"

To our great disappointment, the answer was exactly the same, "Sir, just about five miles."

'Silly people!' we thought.

We decided to ignore their estimate, and we proceeded ahead, thinking that they themselves perhaps had no idea about the distance to the source of the river and marched on.

It was taking too long to go by the regular narrow, winding footpath, and we were getting a bit impatient by now, so we

decided to take a short cut by climbing up on the hill and going down the other side to reach our destination more quickly, avoiding the long winding path around the mountain.

We were just about to reach the top of the hill, when all of a sudden some four or five fierce-looking women approached us with sharp sickles in their hands.

Without any introduction they shouted at us, "How dare you enter our fields! Retreat at once or we will chop your heads off."

We did not even understand their language, but their frightening expression was enough to convey their threat. However, our local servant understood what they were saying.

He said, "Let us climb down the way we climbed up. It is no use arguing with these women."

This encounter with the hill tribeswomen was extremely unexpected – more so because we hadn't seen anything like a field anywhere near – but with fire in those women's eyes we had no choice but to retreat. All the effort of climbing the high hill had been wasted as also the time spent in climbing. Quickly we climbed down as fast as we could and resumed our walk along the narrow, winding, rough, rocky footpath along the edge of the mountain.

By now our New Delhi summer sandals had started getting loose and frayed. Coming fresh from Delhi we had not realised that to go that far we would need proper walking shoes. Our family, like all Mathur families, devoted much more attention to food than to shoes. We too hadn't paid much attention to our shoes.

We trudged on. To our great surprise the hills and valleys became green again with a variety of tall trees. Pine trees were predominant and their dry silky needles were all over the footpath. We had to walk very carefully lest we slip. Cautiously we marched on. Our uncle led the way; behind him was our brother, Mahesh Dada; I was behind him, but at a little distance.

Suddenly I felt a little rustling in the dried pine needles in front of me. I looked down. Horrors! It was a big snake crossing from the mountain to the valley down below. Unintentionally a big shriek came out of my mouth.

Immediately my uncle and brother looked behind and saw the big snake and shouted at me, "Stop!"

My elder sister, Radhe Jiji who was just behind me, also saw the big snake crossing our way. We all froze where we were till the snake disappeared into the vegetation below in the valley. A creepy feeling gripped me: what if more snakes were lurking on our way!

I was feeling frightened and tired by now, especially because of my uncomfortable loose shoes. Actually we all wanted to rest for a while now. It was getting to twelve noon. We had been walking solidly for almost six hours, and we were hot and hungry.

How much further had we to walk? There was no one to tell us. We marched on.

The next hill had much more vegetation on it. We were admiring the sublime scenery of the mighty mountains but by now I was feeling ill at ease and wished I could sit down for a bit. I wanted to enjoy the natural beauty of the mountains and rest my feet! But where was the time to sit and rest? Our destination was still not in sight!

However, it seemed that God had heard my prayer. As soon as we took the turning to the next hill a vast vista of dry, broad space greeted us. It not only looked a safer place than the snake hill but to my great relief we saw a nice, big bench waiting for us there 'God, you are really kind,' I said to myself. 'When I could really not walk any further You provided me with a seat.'

I think we all were happy to see that bench, but we wondered who could have taken the trouble to put such a big bench there? Only our uncle had his misgivings. To the rest of us at that moment it did not matter who had put the bench there and why. All that mattered was that there was at last a comfortable seat to sit on. Not only was the bench inviting but the sight of a small settlement down the valley gave us hope. We felt that the little village must be by the river bank only otherwise how would anybody be living there in that wilderness miles away from any civilization! With great relief, we asked the servant to open up the basket containing the snacks and the fruits. We were all feeling voraciously hungry. I felt as if I could devour all the food that the poor servant had been carrying for us all the way, but we decided that now that we were so near the river we should only have a snack there and have the actual picnic on reaching our destination, which we thought must be just down the hill across the village.

Alas! Our hopes were very short-lived. No sooner had we started munching the goodies, when suddenly we heard the sound of several horses' hooves rushing towards us. God! Who could they be?

My uncle was the first one to guess, and he guessed right too. He asked us to take off our gold bangles and chains immediately, and he hid them in his pockets. Then he asked the servant to pack up everything as quickly as possible. The servant had hardly started packing when a hefty, strongly built, officious-looking person stopped his horse right in front of us and demanded who we were and what were we doing there?

We were taken aback! From where has this giant appeared all of a sudden and why?

My uncle, who was already suspicious, replied politely and truthfully that we were travellers and had come there in search of the source of the River Satluj. "Seeing this bench, we thought we would rest for a bit for a drink of water."

The man roared a mighty laugh. "River Satluj? Forget about it! it is five miles away from here. Come with me to my village. I shall give you some water."

As the chief was talking to us, his followers – all frighteningly strong men with black moustaches, and turbans covering half their faces – some ten or twelve of them, all on horsebacks, passed us by one by one. They glared at us, but, without stopping or speaking a word, they disappeared into jungle along the narrow, single-file path leading to their village in the valley. We stood there holding our breath.

It was all very clear now. They were a band of dangerous dacoits, returning to their village after their night's loot. Their bags were full of stolen stuff, heavily laden on both sides of their saddles, but covered by firewood as if they were woodcutters.

The chief asked us again to follow him to his village, but my uncle politely declined his offer and motioned us to start moving. The dacoit chief threw an indifferent glance at my uncle and galloped off. Our uncle and the servant followed us after making sure that neither the bandit chief nor any of his followers were coming after us.

We were dead frightened after this unexpected encounter with the dacoits. We hastened our steps lest the thieves follow us. To avoid being chased by the dacoits, we did not take the regular narrow path along the hillside but entered into the woods, hiding ourselves as best as we could from the thieves and their den below.

We must have walked at least one more mile down into the thickly forested valley, not knowing exactly where we were going, but soon we felt as if our dream was to come true when we heard the sweet sound of a waterfall nearby and we were exhilarated to see the glimmering, glittering rivulets cascading down from the lofty mountains to the left of us. Oh, what a sight! We stood there spellbound, just admiring the glorious view. Thank God! We were very near our destination long last. Our spirits rose, our hopes were heightened and we hurried forward, eager to touch the water.

Now, after walking a distance of five miles several times over, at last our dream was becoming a reality. Oh! Why all those trees in between?

We were tearing fast among them when suddenly a man, whom we took to be a hermit, materialized in front of us as if by magic. In sheer bewilderment we looked at him and he looked at us. We were as utterly astounded to see him as he was to see us. Perhaps he had never before seen any human being there; we too had certainly not expected to see anyone there. He seemed absolutely taken aback to see us young people in the middle of the thick forest. He approached us and softly asked what were we doing there in that dangerous valley?

"Dangerous? Why?" we asked him.

"Don't you know? This valley is full of wild animals. There are tigers, mountain lions and, worst of all, black bears. Large families of them live here. Retrace your steps at once. It is almost 3.30 now – time for the wild beasts to come out of their hidings in search of food. Return as fast as you can."

"Wild animals?" my brother asked, astonished.

"Yes! Believe me, I am telling you the truth. Now hasten! It is not safe to be here at this time."

A shudder went through my body.

"If it is not safe, then why are you here yourself?" enquired my brother politely.

"Never mind about me – I have made friends with them."

This was the most unexpected of all happenings. Respectfully we said to the hermit that we just wanted to touch the water of the River Satluj which was so close to us now.

"Close?" The hermit smiled at us. The river looks near from here, but it is a good five miles away, down at the very bottom of the densely forested valley. Before you can actually reach the water, there is a very, very slippery dangerous slope down there."

This was the last straw to break our backs. How many five-miles' had we already walked? Now we could clearly see the river cascading down the mountains, but we were told it was still five miles away. Was the hermit really telling the truth, or was he just trying to dissuade us from going any further down? We felt extremely disappointed and disheartened.

Pangs of hunger suddenly assailed us. We were desperately hungry, but we had been postponing our picnic till we reached the water's edge. That dream was suddenly shattered. Now we desperately needed some place to sit down and have something to eat. We had not eaten anything substantial since morning, so we asked the hermit to tell us of some safe place where we could sit down and eat.

"Come to my hut, then. You can sit there and eat and I will also give you water from the River Satluj to drink. And you can take some with you if you want to."

This was a welcome suggestion to our tired souls. He asked us to follow him and led us to his little hermitage.

The cottage was nothing more than a tiny thatched room with a little veranda in front. He told us that we could sit in his veranda and have our lunch there. Our servant spread the mat we had brought with us and laid out our food. We ate the food, but we felt very disappointed at not being able to reach our destination. We had to content ourselves with the sweet, cold Satluj water that the hermit had given us from his hut.

As soon as we had finished eating, the hermit said, "It is dark now. It is not safe for you to go on your own in this forest. Come, I will lead you safely out of this dense jungle."

He led the way for about a mile, or perhaps a bit more, till we reached beyond the haunts of dangerous animals.

Once our nerves were steadied, both my sister, Shanti Jiji,

and myself realized that our sandals were completely torn apart. We tied them to our feet with our three-pronged hair ties, which are called *chutila*. In this way we walked some distance, but soon the *chutilas* also gave way. I dreaded to walk barefoot on the snake hill, so my brother and uncle gave us their UTC socks, which were woollen and very thick. They gave us some relief, but not for too long. After some miles they too started tearing off on those stony, thorny, rough paths. Ultimately my uncle and brother both had to take off their ties so that we could tie our broken sandals over the UTC socks to our feet.

It had become quite dark by now and we were really scared to think that we still had to cross our way back over the snake hill, through the dacoit dens and across the fierce women's fields.

With aching bodies and frightful thoughts we trudged on. I have no idea how we managed to cross all those dreadful hills. Our eyes were looking ahead, searching for the Chota Simla lights.

Before we could glimpse the lights some noises reached our ears. Now who could they be? Another gang of dacoits? Our imaginations were running wild in sheer fright.

Soon we heard, "Hey, Sahib, Sahib!"

We stood still for a moment. Who were they? Whom were they calling? In the dark it was impossible to see any faces distinctly. The voices came nearer and hailed us: "Mathur Sahib – Doctor Sahib, Bhaiyaji!"

Soon we saw two gentlemen in front of us saying, "Thank God! At long last we have found you!"

"Who are you?" my brother asked with as much bravado as he could muster.

"Sir, we are from Engineer Sahib's office. He has sent us in search of you. You know it is past ten o'clock. The Bare Sahib is so worried about you all. He has sent people in all directions in search of you. He is so worried. Come, let us walk fast. Sir is extremely worried."

Though I was relieved after discovering who they were, I couldn't help muttering to myself, 'Our feet are all swollen up – we can't walk fast!'

Anyhow, we now felt much safer and light-hearted in their welcome company and tried our best to hasten our steps. It was past 11 p.m. when at last we reached home.

Father looked at us – half angry, half relieved. He ordered the servants to bring buckets of hot water with salt added and told us to sit with our feet soaking in the hot salty water to reduce the swelling in our feet, while the servants heated up some food.

At home another drama was unfolding.

That evening, when my younger brother and sisters came back from their school, Veena found the opportunity of her life to use Mahesh Dada's air gun. When we older ones were around, she was not allowed to touch it at all.

It was a harmless air gun but more than just a toy. The bullets were tiny, half-centimetre round metallic balls. It could not kill dogs or cats but was enough to shoot down a tiny bird. This we had learnt by experimentation. My brother used it to improve his aim by targeting empty cans. The tiny bullets never went through the tins, but just made tiny little dents in them. It was a fun thing, but it was kept out of the reach of children. That is why the younger children were so keen to lay their hands on it.

Finding none of her elders in the house, the first thing that occurred to Veena was to try the gun. She put a tiny round metallic ball in the muzzle of the gun, put the index finger of her left arm right on the muzzle and 'Bang!' the ball went straight into her finger and comfortably lodged itself there.

When she started crying, then only my *bhabiji* came running to her, but she could not comprehend what to do! Fortunately my father returned from his office soon after and found my sister crying uncontrollably with a red and blue swollen-up finger and the tiny bullet nicely embedded in her finger. She had to be taken to the hospital immediately.

In Simla in those days there was no other mode of transport except 'paroplane', which is walking on foot. My sister had to be taken to the hospital sometimes in my father's arms and sometimes on the servant's back. Simla is spread among the high hills of the Himalayas, and there were no motorable roads there in those days.

Anyway it took the emergency doctors quite some time to take the bullet out and dress up the wound.

It was after returning from the hospital, and finding that we older children were still not back home from our excursion, that my father seriously started worrying about us. He waited for another hour or so and, when there was still no sign of us, he phoned his office people (because there were none of our own family there). He sent three or four parties in different directions in search of us. It was one of these parties that found us and guided us home.

It was past 11 p.m. Though extremely tired, hungry and disenchanted, we had returned, full of unexpected adventures, yet there was a strange urge in our minds to go back to the source of the river and to touch its water some day in the future. However, because of this other incident at home none of us had the courage to ask for permission again from our father.

Thus those elusive five miles have remained as elusive as ever to this day.

P.S. My elder sister Shanti Rani had written this incident in Hindi in 1943 – and was awarded the 1st prize in the All India Essay Competition.

IN BETWEEN A TIGER AND A TIGRESS

Prelude

I have always had a strange fascination towards tigers and lions, maybe because they are so majestic, so awe-aspiring, so magnificently beautiful and so very frighteningly attractive. Yes, attractive of course, but from a distance only. I would be too frightened to go anywhere near them. Anyway, in big cities like Delhi or Bombay, where I used to live, there was no chance of seeing them at close range, except in zoos. I wanted to see them in their natural habitat in jungles near the sparkling tropical waterfalls as shown in the pictures of our Divine Mother, Goddess Ma Durga, riding majestically over them.

I remember going into the thick Rajasthani forests of the state of Udaipur in the middle of the night with my father's colleagues who were fond of big game hunting. All I wanted was to have a glimpse of the lords of the jungle in their natural habitat, but I never had any luck.

However, several years later, after my marriage, I got the opportunity of my life, when we moved to Pune. My husband had joined the Gokhale Institute of Politics and Economics as a professor. He loved his teaching and research work, to which he was totally dedicated. He had only been teaching for a few years when he was made the head of department as well as the director of the institute. It was a nice, dignified job, but a director's job in India is largely administrative, involving too much paperwork, meeting too many people and attending and organising meetings at home and abroad. Now this type of administrative job was not my husband's cup of tea. He desperately wanted to escape from it all at least once a year, even if just for a few days only. He wanted to retreat to a place where there would be no telephones, no telegrams, no letters – no communication with the outside world at all – a place where he could relax in peace and quiet, away from the worries of his administrative job. Finally, just by chance, one day he actually did find such a place.

One evening, when on some special occasion he had gone to the nearby Parvati Temple in Pune, he was surprised to hear a priest chanting prayers in Sanskrit – the language of the Vedas. In most of the temples of Pune, the worship rituals and prayers are sung in the state language of Maharashtra, which is Marathi. That is why he was pleasantly surprised to hear the prayers being sung in Sanskrit that day.

Professor Mathur, my husband, was a great scholar of Sanskrit. He had graduated in Sanskrit and had studied the Vedas in their original script, Sanskrit, as a hobby. He was much impressed with the priest and wanted to talk to him. So he waited just outside the central sanctum of the temple to be able talk to the *panditji* (the priest) after the *puja archana* (the worship ritual) was over.

During their conversation, the priest told my husband that he was not from Pune, or even from any other town in Maharashtra, but from Ayodhya (A town in Uttr Pradesh, North India, the birthplace of Lord Rama). At present he had been invited to serve as the chief priest of the famous Bhimashankar Temple, some hundred miles west of Pune. The temple is situated in a deep valley surrounded by dense forest amidst the Western Ghats, which lie all along the western coast of the Indian Peninsula.

The legend has it that when the famous five Pandavas were banished into exile for twelve years by their ambitious cousin, Duryodhana, they had to spend one year in hiding before returning back to their capital, Hastinapur. It was during this period of hiding that they had travelled to Maharashtra, which in those days was indeed a very remote palace from the seat of their empire at Hastinapur. They hid themselves in the deep densely forested hills and vales of the Western Ghats. The Temple of Lord Shiva was built by Bhima, the strongest of the Pandavas during that period of hiding; hence it got its name, the Bhimashankar Temple (i.e. the temple of Lord Shiva, built by Bhima).

In addition to the temple they built five houses for themselves – one for each of the five Pandavas. The five houses of the five Pandavas and the temple itself are still there, and even now they are not easily visible or accessible. They are built deep down in the thickly forested valley.

Devotees of Lord Shiva know about the temple but very few know its exact location. The *panditji* asked my husband to come and visit the temple some day. What else could my husband want?

In return, my husband also requested the *panditji* to come to our house whenever it was convenient to him. The *panditji* readily accepted our invitation and said that he would come to our house the very next day, which was a Sunday, in the morning because in the afternoon he had to catch the bus back to Bhimashankar. Next day, as promised, he was at our home at about 11 a.m.

My husband and he had lively talks on several religious topics. Both he and my husband got quite keen on our visiting the temple.

I enquired if there were any hotels where we could come and stay with our children?

The *panditji* had a hearty laugh at my question. He said, "Bhimashankar is not a place like Bombay or Pune where hotels abound. In fact," he added, "there is no other building there, except the temple and the five houses of the five Pandavas, where nowadays live the five priests who perform the five-times worship of the Lord in the temple."

When we heard this, a shadow of disappointment descended on our faces. We wondered where were we to stay if there was no place for us to spend the night! The temple was not so near that we could just go and come back the same day by bus. The *panditji* was quick to notice our concern. Immediately he blurted out, "Why do you worry about staying? You shall all be my guests. You will stay with me in my house."

This was more than we could have ever expected of him. However, on his insistence, we accepted his invitation. The *panditji* also added that if we come to Bhimashankar we should come prepared to stay a minimum of one week, because there would be no bus till the following weekend. He told us that there was only one weekly bus service that connected the temple to Pune. The bus from Bhimashankar came on a Saturday and returned on a Sunday. If we decided to return during the week, we would have to walk on foot up to the next village, which was more than a mile further up along the motorable road, on the plateau above the valleys.

After the *panditji* left, we started thinking seriously of going to Bhimashankar for a week during the children's summer vacations. Our children were quite excited to go to a new place for the summer holidays. My husband considered that the remote and solitary location of the temple might be just the ideal place he had been wanting to go ever since the directorship of the institute was loaded on him. It was cut off from the rest of the world and the everyday routine responsibilities of his job. I was just interested in seeing the legendary ancient temple. So it was decided that during the summer vacations that year, which was 1967, we should go to Bhimashankar for a week and accept the *panditji*'s offer of staying as guests in his house.

The children's summer vacations started at the end of April. We decided to go to the temple in the first week of May. Our host, the *panditji*, was accordingly informed on his next weekly visit to Pune. Every week on a Saturday, he and other priests from the temple used to come to Pune to do the necessary shopping for the temple and for their families. They bought matchboxes, kerosene oil to light the lamps at night, sugar and salt, etc. Most of their vegetables and grains and spices they grew themselves on the temple lands. They used to come on a Saturday and return on the following Sunday.

The *panditji* told us that if we forgot anything, then we would have to do without it for the full week because there were no shops around the temple and there was no transport either, so we did our packing carefully trying not to forget anything.

In addition to our clothes we packed a considerable amount of food, including snacks for the children. Most important of all, we packed with great care some *Gangajal* (water from the River Ganges) as an offering for the Lord Shiva himself. (We normally used to keep a bottle or two of the sacred water brought from Benaras or Allahbad – two very sacred cities of India, where the three holy rivers, Ganga, Yamuna and Saraswati, converge.) This sacred water does not get bad or stale even if kept for years. It is almost a must in several religious ceremonies, so almost all Hindu families keep some *Gangajal* in their homes. It is believed that nothing pleases Lord Shiva more than an offering of the sacred water. Hence we saw to it that we didn't forget to take some of it with us.

With great excitement, on the first Sunday of May 1967, we reached the bus stop in good time to catch the two o'clock bus. It was good that we had left a bit early, because otherwise we would not have got seats in the bus. The bus, being the only one and running only once a week, started getting very full very fast.

By the time we actually left Pune it was literally overflowing with passengers and their shopping bags, baskets and bundles of all shapes and sizes. In the heat of the day it got almost suffocating inside. That bus was the only connecting link between several remote villages and Pune, and if passengers missed it, there was no other means by which they could travel to their destinations. Therefore the driver and the conductor had no other choice but to accommodate everyone who needed to go to any of those remote villages.

The ride in the bus started reasonably smoothly, considering the load of passengers it was carrying, but once it left Pune we had a real taste of what it is like to ride on a rough, uneven mud road in an old bus. There were jolts and jerks every minute because of the innumerable potholes. Had the bus been not so tightly packed with passengers and their belongings, some of us would have been literally thrown out of our seats. Anyway, it took us more than four hours to cover a distance of about a hundred miles, not only because the road was rough and winding but also because the bus stopped at every little village it passed through.

At long last, climbing and winding its way up the mountain road, the bus suddenly stopped, seemingly in the middle of nowhere. No bus stop or building was in sight. There was just a comparatively wide and open even space.

The conductor announced, "People for Bhimashankar get down here."

We were aghast. What? Get down in the middle of nowhere

in the thick jungle? No, we were not going to get down there. No way!

The conductor announced again pointing towards us, "People for Bhimashankar get down here."

We were in a dilemma: to get down or not to get down!

Oh, what a relief! We saw our *panditji* rushing towards the bus. So that little clearing was indeed the place to get down for the Bhimashankar Temple. We heaved a sigh of surprised relief.

On getting down from the bus, we noticed that there were three sizeable balls, ranging from about thirty inches to eighty inches in diameter of solid concrete, painted white, lying here and there at some distance to each other. They were definitely handmade, but we could never understand who made them for what purpose or why they were left there. Perhaps they were purposely brought and kept there to indicate to the bus drivers to stop the bus for Bhimashankar passengers. We used to joke that they were seats made for Mother Goddess's lions to rest on. Anyway, our *panditji* greeted us with a warm welcome, helped to take our luggage down from the roof of the bus, offered to carry some of it himself and asked us to follow him.

The footpath to the *panditji*'s house was wide and smooth, bordered on both sides with beautiful flowery shrubs and tall trees. The whole pathway was also littered with curious-looking, tiny green mangoes, only about an inch in diameter. I picked up a few and enquired about them. I was told that they were just wild fruits – not edible at all. How curious everything was! We all enjoyed the unusual greenery and scenery all around. Full of high spirits, the children went jumping and chirping all the way, picking up a flower here and a leaf there. My husband chatted with the *panditji* all the way to his house. It was dusk by the time we reached the gate to the *panditji*'s house.

The *panditji* had carefully prepared the front room of his house for us. It was quite a big, impressive room. He had spread a thick cotton rug on its floor and covered it up with clean white sheets, with pillows for all of us. In one corner he had placed a pitcher of sweet, cold water and some stainless-steel tumblers. In a city such Spartan arrangements would have meant nothing, but in such an isolated place, after the long, tiring bus journey, we felt as if we had been offered the luxury of a palace. As soon as the *panditji* made us comfortable, he opened a door which led to the kitchen. The sweet smell of the ambe mohar rice (a very special local variety of rice which, while cooking, gives off the very fragrant smell of ripe mangoes) filled our nostrils, and the smell of fresh vegetables and herbs made us feel very welcome and hungry indeed. The *panditji* asked us to refresh ourselves in the adjoining bathroom and come straight for dinner, which he had himself prepared and kept ready for us.

Believe me, it was one of the finest dinners we have ever had. It was so simple yet so tasty.

After dinner we all felt like going out for a walk. Being summer, it was still not too dark, but our host firmly said, "No, no, not at this time. Go in the morning." He kept us all engrossed by telling stories about the place.

Soon the children were fast asleep. We too were tired and retired to our princely bed of stone floor covered with a cotton rug and a clean white sheet over it.

In the morning we all got up quite fresh and wanted to go out exploring the area straight after breakfast. The *panditji* warned us that there were no straight roads to anywhere – instead there was a confusing maze of footpaths all around the temple – so we had to be very careful to keep our bearings, so that we could return back safely. Also he said, as a word of precaution, that the jungles around that area were full of wild animals. All sorts of dangerous animals roam about freely over the hills and dales of those forests. We were taken aback! What? Wild animals? How on earth were the priests themselves living there, then? Had they no fear of the dangerous animals attacking them? The *panditji* simply laughed at our questions but explained all the same. He told us with absolute confidence that, up to a radius of one mile, all around the temple was a hallowed area, where the animals could do no harm to the devotees of Lord Shiva. So there was nothing to fear from them.

He walked with us a short distance and showed us a square reservoir of water, perhaps originally built by the Pandavas themselves, where the rainwater was automatically collected. He told us they used that water for cleaning, cooking, washing etc. – only for drinking they get water from the river flowing at the very bottom of the valley. Then he added, "Many times when we need water after dark, we often see the tigers or leopards drinking water from the reservoir. Sometimes they are just a little distance away from us on the same side of the reservoir and sometimes on any other side. We say nothing to them and they do nothing to us. We live in perfect harmony with one another."

We were aghast! What, men and beasts drinking at the same time at the same place from the same source of water! Unbelievable! This was my first mental reaction. It was difficult to believe, but the *panditji*, a man of God, himself was telling us, so there was no question of not believing him, but we had certainly not bargained for it.

It was one thing to go in search of dangerous animals at the reckless young age of eighteen or nineteen, but it was totally different to go knowingly to dangerous spots with small children. Even in those bygone years we used to go fully equipped with guns and ammunition, and quite a lot of manpower expert in the art of big-game hunting, sitting safely inside the strongly built military jeeps. Here in these remote mountains there were no guns or expert hunters or automobiles. For a moment a shiver went through my spine.

My husband teased me: "You always wanted to see wild animals in their natural habitat. Now here is your chance. Why are you feeling so afraid? The priests' families live here. They have no fear of the lions and tigers. Why should you be afraid of them?"

It was a hard task to make him understand my point of view. At that time I was at an age when every danger was a thrill and every encounter an adventure. I had had many dangerous encounters, not only with wild beasts but also with frightening things like ghosts and thieves and snakes. Now it was a different thing with the responsibility of children and a husband. No, no, I did not want to go out and explore the jungle. No way! I was not going out anywhere.

The *panditji* was silently smiling and listening to our argument. In the end he said, "If sister" – (it is an etiquette in India to call a female acquaintance as 'sister' or 'bhabi') – "does not want to go, then please don't go. Instead let me take you to the temple for now."

I may add that initially the *panditji* was not planning to accompany us. He wanted to stay back and prepare our lunch before the eleven-o'clock *arti* (worship), which he had assigned for himself that day. He was quite keen to show the temple to us personally and explain everything about it in detail himself.

Going to the temple sounded a much better proposition than taking the risk of meeting dangerous animals. After all, we had come just for that purpose. So happily we all followed the *panditji* to the temple, not forgetting to take our *Gangajal*.

No sooner had we left the *panditji*'s house, and come out into the open, on the broad, smooth road to the temple, when our nostrils were filled with the fresh, fragrant, cool morning breeze of the forest. The air had such a tranquillising, purifying effect on us that it seemed as if we were transported to a completely different world. It was so quiet and so peaceful. I had never had a feeling of such tranquillity in all my life ever before. As we approached the vicinity of the temple the whole atmosphere seemed filled with divinity. It looked so calm and so serene. We could feel the presence of the Lord everywhere – in the trees, in the building, in the air and in everything else around.

A paved road stretched for about two hundred feet up to the gate of the temple. Just after walking a few yards on it we could see the whole temple right in front of us. We were amazed at the grandeur of the ancient temple, its beauty and its art. How did they build such a grand temple in such a remote inaccessible place in the hoary antiquity? It was simply amazing!

In the inner sanctum of the temple, where Lord Shiva's symbol of power is, we felt as if we were in reality at the Lord's feet, in His own pious palace. The temple and the atmosphere around it had a unique tranquillising effect. Automatically we felt like bowing at His feet. We were very glad that we had brought some precious *Gangajal* to be offered at the feet of the Lord.

My husband poured the sacred water on the Shiv Ling, accompanied by sacred mantras recited by the *panditji*, and our children and I all offered flowers.

After the worship, we were shown around the temple. Every little detail looked so amazing, considering its age.

Once out of the temple, I felt I was a different person. Gone was my fear of all the wildlife. On the contrary, the hills and the dales looked so attractive and tempting as if inviting us to go and explore them. All around the temple and the *panditji*'s house the land had been cleared of tiny, thorny shrubs for about forty-fifty yards. Only the very big trees were left standing on the shiny slopes of golden sands. The giant trees seemed to provide a sort of canopy over our heads as if trying to protect us from the intense heat of the midday summer sun. Who could resist roaming about in such a heavenly, beautiful paradise?

The children loved playing on those smooth sandy slopes. It became our daily routine to go out after breakfast and roam about in the beautiful jungle as freely as the wild animals and inhale the pure air of the divine forest. However, the thought of encountering any wild animal, at any time, at any place, was always at the back of our minds. We had to keep a keen open eye for them. After all, we had our small children with us, and we had to make sure that they did not wander too far away from us. We were continuously on the lookout for any danger lurking around.

On the first day we did not see any animal, big or small, except beautiful little squirrels and several kinds of familiar and unfamiliar birds. We felt exhilarated, excited and quite safe.

Next day we ventured a little further and to our surprise saw a little lad, eleven or twelve years old, tending a herd of cows and little calves all by himself. I could not resist asking him if he was not afraid of the dangerous animals of the jungle. He replied with great confidence that he was not at all afraid of them because he could chase them away or even fight with them with his stick if the need be. That was very brave, I thought, but how about the cattle? Were they safe too?

The boy replied with perfect ease, "Yes, but sometimes when I have not been watchful they have taken away a calf or two in the past."

To him it was just a way of life. We could not help wondering at his statements and his courage!

TELLTALE SIGNS
On the third day we ventured a little further and climbed to the top of the highest hillock. To our surprise we saw some fresh

golden droppings, which we assumed could be of no other animal except lions because all other animals have black or brownish droppings. Moreover, the droppings were on a flat, muddy area with no vegetation at the top of the mountain with a sort of natural low boundary around it. It was evident that that particular spot on the hilltop was a favourite haunt of the king of the animals – lions. Hurriedly we took a glance around to make sure that none were lurking nearby. Fortunately we did not see any at all as far off as the eye could see.

As I think about it now, it seems very strange that though we knew there were wild animals all over those hills and dales we somehow rarely felt any fear of them. We continued with our wanderings, enjoying the serene, majestic beauty of the mountains, totally fearless, unarmed and unharmed, all through the mornings and also in the bright sunny afternoons. Only in the evenings we did not have the courage to go out. It seemed a bit too risky to take chances with tigers and lions in the evenings, when they come out in search of food.

One day, we took the children out in the morning after breakfast and, as usual, returned for lunch. After lunch, when the children were having a midday nap, my husband said, "Let us leave the children in the safety of the house and in the care of our host *panditji* and walk down to the river." We had not seen the river so far, because we were a bit apprehensive to go in the deep, dense, dark valley with the children. It was by God's grace that we had not faced any dangerous situation so far, but who could say about the future! It was best not to take any foolish risks. On the hilltops in the bright daylight it was one thing, but in the cool, dark, shady places it was different. The lions and tigers might be there, by the river, for a drink of water or just to relax in the cool shade under the trees. But my husband was very keen to see the river and so was I, so just the two of us quietly slipped out of the house, after getting an OK signal from the *panditji*.

Now, as we started wending our way down the valley, we felt under our feet a thick carpet of dried fallen leaves, which made a peculiar 'churr murr' sound as we walked over them. This aroused a new fear now – that of snakes lying hidden under the foliage! I am morbidly afraid of snakes. I can face a tiger but not a snake. What should we do? Should we turn back or should we proceed further? The thought of seeing the river, which we thought was just a few more feet down, proved to be greater than our fear of snakes, so we pushed on cautiously. After trudging down another thirty or forty feet we still saw no sign of the river. I was too afraid to go down any further. It was quite dark there even at midday. The sun's rays did not quite penetrate through the thick canopy of fresh green leaves on the gigantic trees. In the end we abandoned our plan and retraced our steps.

When we were nearing the summit of the mountain, we heard heavy footsteps coming from the other side. We surmised that it must be two woodcutters bringing down a heavy load of wood on their heads for the temple, so we anxiously waited to see them in the good hope of finding more about the place. But suddenly the sound of the footsteps stopped. We looked at each other in astonishment. What had happened? Why had the heavy footsteps stopped so suddenly? Why were the woodcutters not showing up?

Then suddenly a strong smell coming from that side made it all clear. They were not the steps of woodcutters, but the heavy thumps of the king of the forest, the great lion. The big thing had perhaps seen us from the top of the hill but we had not seen him. He had perhaps sat down to hide himself from us. Perhaps he was as apprehensive of us as we were of him. We had not seen him, but we could feel his presence. We knew he was sitting right at the edge of the mountain on the top of the hill. As soon as the realisation dawned upon us, all our fearlessness evaporated in thin air. God save our souls! Run! Run! Run!

With speed and caution we retraced our steps as quietly and as quickly as we could, hiding and fleeing at the same time, away from the apparent danger. But there could still be danger from other wild beasts lurking in those densely forested mountains. Danger could be just about anywhere – in front of us, at our back or on our sides. We just had to be very very alert and cautious. Panting and perspiring, we pushed on. At long last, a glimpse of the temple steeple shimmering in the setting sun from behind the trees rewarded our efforts. Still there was no time to rest or relax! We had to continue till we reached the *panditji*'s house. Totally breathless, panting and throbbing, we made it, though still shivering from the shock and the thought that the great lion might yet be behind us.

Seeing us in that frightened and exhausted condition, the *panditji* could guess that we had been in some trouble. He, with our children, had been anxiously waiting for our return. They had all been worrying. We had told them we should be back in a little over an hour. It was nearing three hours now. The children were on the verge of crying, and the *panditji* had been having a hard time keeping them quiet and entertained.

As soon as they saw us they ran to us. We hugged them warmly and lovingly, glad to be with them again.

When we had regained our breath, the *panditji* asked us what had happened. Why were we looking so frightened? Had we had an encounter with any wild beast? When we narrated our narrow escape, the *panditji* got a bit serious and told us that on our way back we had wandered on a totally different trail, which was opposite to the temple as well as to his house. That hill was out of the radius of the sanctity of the temple. We were taken aback! How could that be? How had we gone so drastically wrong? Perhaps the ghostly darkness of the dense valley, added to our fear of snakes and other dangerous creatures, had clouded our power of straight thinking and we had gone desperately astray.

THE SLEEPING BEAUTY

Next day, our enthusiasm for wanderings was subdued quite a bit, but the call of the jungle was too great to resist. Moreover, what would we do sitting all day inside the *panditji*'s house? So we decided to go into the jungle anyway, but stay close to the temple. Once out of the house, the fear vanished from our minds as usual and we felt deeply soaked in the serene beauty of the divine hills.

Our children thoroughly enjoyed themselves chattering and singing and running about in the open green woodlands. We too were trying to make the best of the last day of our holiday. (Next day we had to take the bus back to Pune.)

We were on our way back on the narrow footpath when suddenly a strong gust of wind brought the strong smell of some wild animal nearby. We looked around and saw, to our sheer horror, a tigress sleeping silently on the slope of the hill, hardly twelve feet away from us. We were too thrilled to worry or exclaim, but, hanging on to dear life, both my husband and I put our fingers on our lips and motioned the children to be absolutely quite. We had to be extremely cautious lest the tigress woke up and leapt on us. It was a critical but thrilling situation – something to remember.

The fear of encountering deadly poisonous snakes lurking on those slopes was also never far away.

On our return to Pune, the news of our visit to the sacred Bhimashankar temple and our close encounters with the wildlife spread quickly among all our acquaintances, friends and relatives. Now everybody wanted to go to see the temple and witness the wildlife around it for themselves. We had requests from so many people to take them with us on our next trip to the fascinating place. However, next year we had to abandon our plan of visiting the temple because my husband could not take any time off during the children's summer vacations due to pressure of work at the institute.

On hearing about the abandoning of our programme to go to Bhimashankar, one of my husband's cousins, who also lived in Pune with her family, insisted that we go with them just for one day in their four-wheel-drive van. It would take a maximum of about two and a half hours each way and we could easily go and come back the same day in her big van. She is a lady of firm determination; no pleas prevailed with her. She was determined to see the temple and, more than the temple, the tigers. We had to give in to her persistent requests. Much to her disappointment, the day trip with her was quite uneventful – no sightings and no traces of any animals of any kind. Boring!

In June 1969, my nephew from Jaipur was visiting us after his final school exams. He had been hearing of our adventures in the enchanted forests around the temple for the past two years. Now he too wanted to go and see the place himself. As a matter of fact, we were all quite keen to visit the temple again.

Only one thing was in the way. Earlier that year I had to undergo major abdominal surgery. My father and elder brother, Dr T. G. Mathur, who was a senior surgeon at the Sawai Mansingh

Hospital in Jaipur at that time, had called me to their place for surgery. Some complications had arisen after the operation and I had to stay in Jaipur till the end of April. By the time I came back I was feeling more or less normal and fit enough to carry on with my everyday routine light housework again.

The talk of going to Bhimashankar made me feel fit again. Apart from my own family, everybody else was totally against my taking such an excursion. Their main argument was that after such a major operation I should not be sleeping rough on the hard floor of the *panditji*'s house. Moreover, we were ourselves a bit hesitant to take our guest nephew to a place where he would not get the comforts he was used to. Perhaps we could ask our host *panditji* to provide a bed for him at least, but that did not seem right. We looked at all the pros and cons of such an excursion. But the children were insistent and, most of all, was our nephew.

Our next-door neighbour and family friend, Mr Chandras, who was a forest officer, suggested that if our nephew and children were really so keen on going to Bhimashankar, then he could do one thing. He could ask the forestry department to open up the forest dak bungalow (a house reserved for the government officials) for us. He told us that the dak bungalow was fully furnished with comfortable beds, easy chairs and dining chairs, together with the rest of the paraphernalia. Moreover, there were four sturdy servants permanently posted there. They would look after us, do our cooking, cleaning and everything else, and we would be able to live there much more comfortably than in the *panditji*'s house. That seemed a reasonable proposition.

The only hitch was that the forest bungalow was far away from the temple on another hill. There was no guarantee of safety from the wild beasts and going to the temple every day would be impractical for me. Climbing down from the dak bungalow, up to the temple and back again to the dak bungalow would be too much strain on my still weak muscles. Besides, we would have to take our own precautions to protect ourselves from the abundant wildlife there.

Our neighbour, Chandras Sahib, cautioned us about three more things: First, we should never venture outside the bungalow after dusk. Second, we should never throw any food out from the windows, especially any meat, because throwing out food of any kind was like throwing out an invitation to the forest predators. Third, we should never sleep at night with doors and windows open, however hot we may feel inside.

The charm of going to Bhimashankar was so great that no threat of wild animals or discomfort deterred us from going. In our excitement to be able to visit the temple and the enchanted forests again, we accepted all the conditions and suggestions.

With great enthusiasm we took the bus for Bhimashankar, and arrived at our familiar bus stop in the middle of nowhere. Forestry department people and our old friend the *panditji* were all there to receive us.

The climb up to the dak bungalow proved to be a real ordeal for me, and it was out of question for me to do so every day. The result was that I could not go to the temple at all – which was my main interest. I pleaded with my husband every day to take me at least once to the temple. He kept on saying that he would take me to the temple on the day of our return, when I would have to come down anyway to take the bus. He said we would start early after breakfast, go straight to the temple, have the darshan and be back in time for the two o'clock bus. I had no choice but to agree to his decision.

Every day my husband with our children and my nephew used to go in the mornings for the darshan (a glimpse of the god) at the temple and in the afternoons for walks in the fascinating jungle or again to the temple.

Much to my consternation, all six days I had to spend practically the whole day inside the dak bungalow with my little daughter, Shri Nidhi, and my maidservant, whom we had taken with us from Pune. During the day, when everybody was inside, we used to open the doors and the windows for some time to let some fresh air in. The four servants of the forestry department used to guard the bungalow on all four sides. That was the only time my daughter and I could come out and enjoy the serene lush green beauty of the enchanting forest. There was sufficient open space outside the bungalow for children to play and put the easy chairs out and enjoy the scenery all around. A pleasant breeze blew all the time on the hilltop, so the summer Sun never seemed too hot there.

On the eve of our departure, I was inside the bungalow with my little daughter and my maidservant. The others had gone out on their customary ramblings. Usually they would go out by about four and come back by about six in the evening, but that day they were very late. It was past seven in the evening and getting dark. We were getting very worried. No longer could we sit inside. All three of us came out, in spite of the servants yelling at us not to do so because it was the time when the lions and tigers come out in search of their food. But what did our safety matter when the rest of our family was still out there in the wild forest? My eyes were fixed on the hazily visible footpath on the comparatively even ground between the temple hill and the start of ascent to the dak bungalow – the way they were supposed to come back. The daylight was fading into darkness and it was getting darker.

In the dusky twilight I saw to my horror some wild animal crossing that very footpath on which my family had to return. My fears knew no bounds. I was extremely worried. Seeing me in that condition and refusing to go inside, the servants lit big fires on all the four sides of the bungalow to keep the wild animals at bay and pleaded with us to go inside the bungalow. But all their pleas were in vain. We would not go in. We stood there outside the bungalow waiting for our family to return safely. The servants realised that we were not going to listen to them, so two of them came and sat beside us with big bamboo sticks in their hands and two servants went down to look for my husband and children, who they thought would not be safe on their own in the dark. Waiting seemed endless.

At long last the cheerful voices of the children were heard. We heaved a sigh of relief. By God's grace they were all not only safe and sound but very cheerful as well.

Half angry, half happy, crying with relief I enquired in anguish where had they been? Why were they so late?

With great enthusiasm, all of them started bubbling at the same time about the new place – a beautiful lake –that they had discovered. All of them were so eager to tell all about their new adventure in the hitherto unvisited territory beyond the distant hills that it was difficult to understand any of them clearly.

My husband quietened them all down and started describing

how they had discovered a beautiful lake beyond the yonder hills. He told us how beautiful and fertile the area looked with exotic flowers growing all around it. I was still not quite recovered from my shock and worry, so none of his descriptions impressed or interested me, but he went on: "Tomorrow you have got to come with me to see it for yourself." The children were echoing the same thing with one voice.

I turned my head and said, "Nothing doing! I am not going anywhere except to the temple, where I must go and he must take me, according to his promise."

Very consolingly my husband said, "Yes, certainly I will take you to the temple, but before that you have got to come to see the lake and the area around it."

I retorted, "Why? What for? I don't want to see anything – just take me to the temple."

My husband, however, insisted on my going to see the lake and the area around it, because somewhat confidingly he told me that he wanted to buy the whole of that land.

Aghast I said, "Buy land in that remote godforsaken place full of wild beasts?"

"Yes," he replied very calmly, and continued, "the area around the lake looks very fertile and promising; and if we could buy it, then we could start cultivating cashew nuts on a commercial scale there. But you have got to go and see the land for yourself first."

What could I say? If he had set his mind on it, he was going to do it.

I agreed on one condition only: that we should not be late to reach the temple for the eleven-o'clock *Arti*.

Very confidently he told me that there should be no problem with that, because he had seen a short cut, a footpath, which led straight from the lake to the temple.

"Fine," I said. "In that case, I will go to see the lake and the land you want to buy."

With gusto, he outlined the plan: "We must all get ready by 7 a.m; finish breakfast and packing by 7.30 a.m; reach the bus stop with all our luggage by about eight; leave the luggage with our servant girl at the bus stop; and then proceed straight for the lake. It should take us about thirty-five to forty minutes to reach the lake. We can stay at the site for about half an hour or so to examine the potential of the land as a viable proposition for the cultivation of cashew nuts and to enjoy the unspoilt beauty of the lake and it's surroundings. Then, at about 9.30, we will head straight for the temple via the footpath we discovered yesterday. That way we could do both the things – see the lake and attend the *Arti*."

The plan seemed practical enough. I consented to go to the lake but in my heart I had a creepy feeling – an actual fear of the tigers and the other dangerous animals that lived in abundance there. Would it be wise to go there with our four small kids and our guest nephew? My husband understood my predicament, but he consoled me by saying that he had seen several villagers going up and down on those hills last evening. He thought that perhaps the lake was the sole source of water for the surrounding villages, so the place was neither so isolated nor so dangerous as I was imagining. He felt quite safe to go there. To me, our potential for putting ourselves in utmost dangerous situations seemed endless, but God's grace was always greater.

Next morning we started the day as planned. We reached the bus stop by about 8.15, and started off for the lake immediately. We were running a bit late, but it did not seem to matter much because everybody was in high spirits and by quickening our pace a bit we would make up for the time lost. The three boys (our nephew, Ajai, about seventeen years old, and our two sons, Dnyanesh, about fifteen years, and Rajul, about thirteen) and our elder daughter, Shalini, about eleven years old, were enjoying the walk the most. Chattering, jumping, laughing and singing, they were sort of leading the way, totally oblivious of any danger that might be lurking behind the trees, around the hills, or in fact anywhere. My husband had to shout from time to time to stop them from getting too far ahead of us. We had to be a bit slow because our youngest daughter, Shri Nidhi, who was only about four years old at that time. She could not walk as fast as the others and needed to be carried in our laps from time to time. My pace, because of the operation, was quite slow even otherwise. Moreover, instinctively my eyes were continuously looking around for any hidden danger in those wildlife infested hills. Safety was paramount in my mind.

Still, as we approached the vicinity of the lake, the abundance of natural scenic beauty took over my heart and soul, and for a time I forgot all about the possibility of encountering any danger. Bathed in the glorious early morning sunshine, inhaling the fragrant fresh air of the virgin forest, soon we found ourselves standing at the edge of the lake.

My goodness, what a view! We literally seemed to have been transported from earth to heaven in a jiffy. The beauty of the exotic flowers growing by the side of the lake surpassed the beauty of any flowers I had ever seen before. What abundance of colours! What vivid variety of nature's wonders! What flowers of such extraordinary beauty and variety! I can't really describe the heavenly beauty of the whole serene place. The bright red lotuses standing high above the surface of the shimmering blue lake amidst the big plate-like green leaves decorated with pearls of dewdrops on them seemed to make the whole place absolutely magical like an enchanted fairyland.

No wonder my husband and children had been so fascinated with it on the previous evening. My husband told me that, yesterday evening with the rays of the setting sun spreading their crimson veil over the sleepy lake had made it look even more enchanting.

I could have spent the whole day there. But, alas! it was our last day there and we had to reach the temple before the eleven-o'clock *arti* and the darshan of the Deity, and we needed to be back in time for the bus after the prasad (lunch). Reluctantly we had to turn back to reach the temple in time for the *arti*.

FACE TO FACE

After walking for about fifteen minutes or so, we reached the spot where the mud road widened a bit and the narrow foot path to the temple started. Happy and quite carefree, my husband led the way along the canopied footpath, holding our elder daughter Shalini's hand in his hand. Then went my older son followed by the younger one, then my nephew and last of all myself with my little daughter in my lap. The footpath was too narrow for all of us to walk side by side.

As I started walking on the narrow path I realised that it was not a straight path at all. It took a sharp turn every ten to twelve feet, and the result was that I could not see any of my family gone in ahead of me. I could only hear their thrilled cheerful voices rejoicing at every little new thing they came across. My nephew was comparatively nearer to me, but not even he was close enough to be seen from where I was. My husband must have marched much further ahead because I could not hear him or my elder daughter at all.

Feeling on top of the world, with the children jumping and enjoying themselves, I was hoping to be at the shrine in time for puja and *arti*. However, as I have stated earlier, though we enjoyed every minute of our wanderings in the wild forests, yet my ears and eyes were always alert and on the look out for any hidden dangers.

Now, as I came to the third turning of the zigzag path, I felt that there was a huge full-grown tiger sitting behind the thick trunk of a huge tall tree as if trying to hide himself from the unknown, unpredictable intruders. I could see its long erect ears, wide piercing eyes and big black moustache on his big frightening face as it rested its head on its folded front feet. I thought that because I had always been thinking of tigers I was making a tiger out of nothing else than the shadow of the big leaves falling on a mound of mud under the tall tree. If it was a real tiger, how was it that nobody else gone in before me had seen it? After all, they had all gone along the very same path just a few moments ago. Surely it must all be in my imagination only. Thus convincing myself I tried to dismiss the idea from my head and proceeded forward.

When I reached the end of the fourth zigzag, where there was a crossroad of jungle paths, I found my nephew standing with a stick in his hand waiting for me anxiously.

As soon as he saw me he said in a sort of commanding voice, "Bhuaji, I won't let you go in a step further."

Astonished, I asked him, "Why?"

He said, "Because, a tiger and a tigress have gone on that very path not very long ago in the same direction as we were coming from. Look at these paw prints," he continued. "They are very fresh and very big – certainly of a full-grown tiger and a tigress. Have a look at these yourself. They are clearly visible in this dry sand."

No doubt I could see some paw-prints in the sand, but I could not say for sure that they were of a tiger and a tigress, as my nephew was saying. I was not quite ready to believe him, so asked him again, "What makes you think that they are of a tiger and a tigress only? They could be of any other wild animal roaming there."

He, a mere lad of sixteen or seventeen, said with great confidence, "No, Bhuaji, I recognise tiger's paw-prints very well. I can assure you that they are of no other animal but a tiger and a tigress only. One set is bigger and the other set is smaller. The bigger ones are of a tiger and the smaller ones are of the tigress. They are intact, which means that they passed along that path just a little while ago."

Hearing him speak so confidently, I asked him to come back with me and look to his right. I showed him the thing I thought was a big tiger trying to hide himself from us.

He looked at it and swallowed a shriek. Frightened he muttered, "Yes, Bhuaji, yes! What else! It surely is a full-grown ferocious tiger. Bhuaji, run! Run, Bhuaji, run. Run fast! Let us get out of this place fast."

When I heard this from him, the earth below my feet seemed to slip away. In sheer terror I quickly handed over my little daughter to him and asked him to run as fast as he could towards the bus stop.

He held on to my arm, and said, "Bhuaji, you come too. Don't stand here!"

Thus saying, he started dragging me.

We had hardly come to the end of that zigzag when lo and behold! What did we see? The tigress, full front, face-to-face, hardly three feet from us. Only a few dry reeds like the thin, yellow stems of dried-up brambles were between us. They were no protection, or partition. She perhaps thought that she has hidden herself from us behind them, but of course it was not so. We could see her whole brownish-black and yellow stripey big body quite clearly. She could perhaps see us much better with her head high above the stunted dry reeds. It seemed that she had run in and then, out of curiosity, had turned back to see who the intruders were. That is perhaps why her face was towards us, and why she happened to be so close. It was an unbelievable situation. Face-to-face with a tigress at such a close range, and the tiger just about ten or twelve feet away on the other side of the path!

Horrors! What were we to do? Should we run? Should we shout? How could we save ourselves from that unbelievable predicament? Trapped by the tiger on the left and the tigress in front! How could we get out of there? Who would listen to us in that godforsaken place even if we shouted for help?

I had already entrusted my youngest daughter to my nephew. Now I handed over my camera too, lest the tigress might take it to be a weapon against her. I implored my nephew to run helter-skelter towards the safety of the bus stop. My nephew wanted me to come out too, but that of course was out of the question. How could I come out when all the rest of the family was still trapped inside the forest? I begged him to run – run as fast as he could for his dear life and for my little daughter's sake. Speechless, he obeyed.

Now I was standing all alone face-to-face with the tigress, and the tiger was not far away on my left. What a strange, frightening situation! The first reaction on the part of both of us – the tigress and me was strangely not one of fear but of sheer amazement. I had always wanted to see the tigers in their natural habitat but definitely not from such a close range and certainly not face-to-face. For quite some time neither she nor I knew how to react. Bewildered, she stared at me and I at her. Perhaps she was a bit amused to see me – only an insignificant creature.

I admired her majestic beauty. Eye-to-eye we both stood motionless for some time.

Once the first reaction of astonishment was over, it did not take me long to realise that her initial apprehension was slowly turning to frustration. I could clearly see it in her eyes. She looked threateningly at me as if warning me to get out of her way. I would have been too glad to do so had my family not still been inside the jungle. I had no other choice but to keep standing there, with my eyes fixed on hers.

Losing her patience, her fierce eyes on mine, she restlessly started moving her whole body from side to side. She looked straight towards me and her eyes penetrated mine as if saying, "How dare you cross my path! Get out of my way?"

I knew for sure that however dangerous the situation was I could not take my eyes from hers even for a second. I knew that as soon as I took my eyes away from hers she would either attack me or join her partner, and then they would start moving back along the path on which my family was. Although the situation was indeed critical and dangerous, God gave me the courage to face it. I gathered all my wits and shouted to my family as loud as I could, "Come back! Come back soon!"

My sons heard my call and returned from wherever they were. My younger son came first. In a hushed tone I asked him to have a quick look at the tigress right in front just behind the dry reeds and run as fast as he could towards the bus stop. He threw a frightened glance at the tigress and ran helter-skelter away from her towards the road. After a while my older son appeared. To him I gave the same instructions in hushed monosyllables. He had already anticipated that there was some danger, so he quickly threw a fleeting glance at the tigress and ran as fast as he could. I was again alone face-to-face with the tigress, waiting for my husband and daughter to emerge out from the jungle.

Waiting was eternity! Why were my husband and daughter not coming out? Did they not hear my call to return back? Where were they? Why were they not coming out? Why were they still in? My impatience was turning into real fright now. I could clearly feel that the tigress was getting ready to strike. She was getting more and more restless. I could see her eyes getting red-hot with rage and she was preparing to attack. She stopped swaying her body from side to side and stood steady with her tail erect. I moved a bit further from her without letting my eyes stray from hers even for a fraction of a second. I knew for sure that as soon as I would take my eyes from hers she would attack me, or maybe she would just come out and join her partner and the two together would be a formidable force. I had to stop that happening at any cost to save my daughter and my husband, who were still somewhere inside the jungle. I had to gather every grain of strength left in me. So instead of going out towards the bus stop I went a little further inside the forest and again shouted desperately, as loudly as I could, "Come back! Come back soon! Come back fast!"

It was evident that on hearing unfamiliar human voices the tiger couple, who were perhaps out for their morning walk on their own personal private path, had become a bit nonplussed and confused by the loud, happy outpourings of the intruders – us, my family, my children. In a hurry to hide themselves from the approaching unknown danger they had steered clear, each hiding in the nearest spot they could jump to on their side of the path. Perhaps they were as apprehensive of us as we were of them. The natural instinct of safety and the urgency of the situation had made them jump to the nearest side and hide. The tiger had plunged to his side and the tigress to her side of the footpath and we were now flanked on both sides by them.

To me, the ferocious face of the tigress and her angry gaze was like being face-to-face with the Devil or Death itself. Still I could not move myself away from her; nor could I move my eyes from hers. Eye-to-eye I stood motionless hoping that my husband and daughter would come out of the jungle soon. Time was running out fast for our safety. The tigress had not actually pounced upon me but she was devouring me with her big ferocious eyes all the time.

I had no other choice but to keep staring at her eyes so that she would not dare to come out of her make-believe hiding. She was looking real ferocious. I could feel that if I did not remove myself from her way she was going to give me a good strong slap, which would make a good juicy morsel of me straight into her partner's jaws. She was getting more deadly by the second, but what could I do? I could not move away till my husband and my daughter would come out of the jungle. To placate her, I had to move a bit but I moved towards inside the jungle not outside, gathered up all my remaining strength and courage and once again I shouted as loudly as I could, "Come back, come back soon, fast, fast, fast."

This time, fortunately, they heard my call and after about five or six minutes or so they appeared on the footpath, dreadfully pale and trembling with fear. I tried to show them the tigress. I pleaded with my husband, "Have at least a quick glance at the tigress," but he wouldn't look. Instead, perspiring and panting, he started dragging me forcefully out of the place. I was mystified. Here I was standing bravely between the tiger and the tigress for so many long minutes and he was so much out of his wits as to not even dare to have a brisk look at her.

Frightened and frustrated, he practically dragged me and my elder daughter out of the narrow tiger path.

Once out of the way of the tigers, with worried watery eyes in utter despair and distress, he muttered, "The boys, the boys – where are they? Have you seen them? I couldn't find them. I have searched everywhere, but could not find them." Still looking all around, he continued, "I hope they are safe. I thought they were just behind me, but on turning back I could not see them. I have searched all the footpaths in this part of the jungle for them."

I said, "Why, they came out of the jungle quite some time back."

"Have they?" He looked at me in disbelief, but heaved a sigh of relief.

"Yes, of course they have," I told him. "On realising that we were trapped between the tiger and the tigress, I called you all to return fast from wherever you were. The boys heard my call and returned; only you and Shalini did not come out."

He looked very perplexed but at the same time a bit relieved. Still not quite out of his distress, he still kept on dragging us towards the bus stop.

At long last we reached the comparative safety of the bus stop. When my husband saw the boys for himself he took a deep breath to relieve himself of the anxiety which was overpowering him. He seated himself on one of the trunks, his heart still throbbing from his ordeal and anxiety.

In a distressed tone he said, "Do you know where I had been?"
"Have you been to the temple already?" I asked angrily.
"No, I have been to the den of those very tigers."
I was taken aback. "What?" I asked in amazement.
"Yes," he said, "what I thought to be the short cut to the temple was actually the tiger path leading straight to their den."
"But how did you know that it was the den of the tigers?"
"Because," he said, "the path ended at the den only. It did not go anywhere further and there was a strong smell of tigers inside. Also, the grass inside the den was freshly pressed, which meant that they had left the den just a little while ago." He continued: "As soon as I realised that the footpath was not a footpath to the temple at all, but a path to the tigers' den, I turned back post haste. I was sure that my sons were following me, but, not seeing them anywhere in the vicinity, I got the fright of my life. My heart sank and a chill went through my spine. Had the tigers taken away my boys? In sheer panic I looked for them everywhere, but in searching for them in the maze of tiger paths I lost my own way. I wandered here and there without being able to find either the children or my own way out."

It was only when my husband heard my desperate last loud calls to them that he got an idea of the direction and came out as fast as he could with my daughter.

We all heaved a sigh of relief. Our throats were parched because of the panic and running about in the heat of the day. Fortunately we had a container of cold water with us. Our servant girl poured water for all of us into our picnic glasses but she was extremely angry with us for not taking her with us.

"Why did you not take me with you?" she demanded. "I wanted to see the tigers too."

Somehow we had to pacify her.

Now we looked at our watches. It was nearing quarter to eleven. We had not realised that we had been in the jungle with the tigers for so long. I had not dared to remove my eyes from the tigress even for a second to look at the time on my wristwatch lest she may come out and block our passage. My husband was too busy looking for the boys to look at his watch. At long last by God's grace we were all out of the danger now!

Perhaps a bit late for the eleven-o'clock *arti*, but if we could walk a bit fast, we might just be able to make it. Even if we missed it we had to go to the temple to thank the Lord for saving us from a really dreadful, dangerous situation.

On our way to the temple we saw a priest hurriedly pacing towards us. As soon as he saw us he called aloud, "Babuji, where were you? Why are you so late? The *arti* is just about to start. The head priest is waiting for you. He is getting worried and he has sent me to look for you. Come, fast! It is already late for the *arti*. Everything is getting delayed. Come quick."

By the time we reached the gate of the temple the bells had already started ringing. We were just in time to join in the prayers, which we did from the bottom of our hearts. The blissful, benevolent, soothing song of the *arti* had never sounded sweeter.

Once the rituals were over, the *panditji* came straight to us with the prasad. With serious concern he enquired, "What was the matter? Where had you gone? Why are you all looking so pale and frightened?"

My husband narrated the whole story of our wandering off to see the lake and how on our way back we had ended up in the tiger's den, taking the tiger path to be a short cut to the temple. He told the *panditji* how, on turning back and not seeing the boys, he had wandered all over in search for them and had lost his own way in the maze of the tiger paths in the dense forest. He also narrated my encounter with the tigers and how I had stood between the tiger and the tigress for almost twenty-five minutes or so.

Panditji heard the story in rapt silence. Then in a very sober tone he said, "Oh, why did you not tell me that you wanted to go to the lake? If only you had told me, I would have sent somebody with you. You know it was not at all safe for you to go there on your own with children, especially because that area was out of the sanctity of the temple." He thanked the Lord for saving us and offered the special prasad he had prepared for us. Then he gave us some extra to take with us to Pune.

We then had to rush fast to catch our bus. The *panditji* accompanied us up to the bus stop and, after making sure we were comfortably seated and all our luggage was put in nicely, he waved farewell as the bus started on its journey back to Pune. At Pune throngs of people came and wanted to touch our feet.

The news of our visiting Bhimashankar during the summer vacations had spread far and wide. We had visited the holiest of the holy places. They tried to touch our feet in reverence, believing that as we had been so near to the deity we might have brought some divinity with us. We were happy to distribute the prasad we had brought with us.

To them our encounter with the tiger and the tigress was very interesting and entertaining but for me it was nothing of the sort. For months on end, whenever I closed my eyes, the frightening, penetrating gaze of the tigress, with which I had stood eye-to-eye for what seemed to be an eternity, would come before my eyes. My sleep was totally ruined. I had nightmares of the scene for a long, long time. The dreadful close encounter with the tiger and the tigress haunted me day and night for months. Then one day I decided to write it all down. Only after I had finished writing did I get some relief from the nightmares I was having.

Originally I wrote down the incident in Hindi, our language, in 1969 itself. It is only recently that I have tried to jot it down in English for the sake of my English friends, almost thirty-five years later. Memory gets misty over the years, but it did not in this case. Every scene is as fresh in my memory still as it was on that eventful day.

POSTSCRIPT

My elder daughter, Shalini, has faint memories of the place and the incident. She wanted to go there again. She went in November 2006 with her husband. To her great dismay and disappointment the whole place has completely changed. Instead of the three big concrete balls to indicate the bus stop, there is a regular bus stop and a big car park with plenty of cars and buses going and coming all the time. The barren road from the bus stop to the temple is flanked on both sides by shops selling all types of things. The isolated hidden temple is now like any other commercialised temple and it is visited by innumerable pilgrims all year round. Maybe the tigers have been hunted away. The jungle has not remained untouched by modern expansion, but has given way under the pressures of the surging population explosion.

THE SUGAR-EATER

"*Yaar, Purushottam*! This won't do. No excuses now. You had promised that you would come to stay with us when Bhabiji will return back from Jaipur." Before my husband could reply, Mr Purang looked at me and continued, "You know, Bhabiji, before we moved to Delhi there was hardly a day when we did not see each other, but now months pass by before he even thinks of us."

My husband interrupted and said, "Don't believe him. He is only trying to pull my leg. The fact is that now he himself has no time for me. He is very busy showing Kundaji around Delhi. So many times I have been to his house, but he is never there. Sometimes he goes to see a picture, sometimes on a picnic, sometimes shopping or whatever."

"No, no, Bhabiji, that's not true – ask him how many times we have invited him to our house but he will not come. He always makes one excuse or another. Now, the latest was that he would come when you would come back from Jaipur. Now that you are here, I am not going to listen to any more excuses."

That was my first real introduction to my husband's closest friend, Mr Ram Gopal Purang, and his wife, Kundaji. They had invited us for lunch along with some other mutual friends, so that I could become acquainted with their circle of close friends. Some of them were already married and some were still in the queue. Kunda Bhabi and Purang Sahib were the senior-most of them all, having been married for the longest time – two years. Others had comparatively new brides. They were a jolly lot. After a hearty meal and bursts of laughter, they all started leaving one by one.

We were the last to take our leave, but Mr Purang would just not let us go. He kept on insisting that now that we were there we should stay with them for at least a few days. We had neither come prepared for that nor had we asked permission of my sister-in-law, my husband's elder sister with whom we were living at that time.

Mr Purang, however, was very insistent. He said, "Don't worry about Jiji. I will explain it all to her when we meet her next; and there's no need to worry about clothes either – we have shared them before and we can share them now."

I was listening to their pleasant arguments with interest. Then I looked at Kunda Bhabi. Her eyes looked as pleading as her husband's. We could not say no to such a loving and earnest invitation.

"OK, agreed," my husband said, shaking his friend's hand tightly. "We shall come at the first possible opportunity, but for now we have got to go."

Ever since our marriage I had been hearing a lot about Mr Ram Gopal Purang and his wife, Kunda. I had met them briefly at the time of our marriage, but at that time I met so many new people in such a short time that I really didn't come to know anybody closely. However, in just three or four months I had learned quite a lot about them. Mr Purang and my husband had been the best of friends from their very early childhood. They belonged to the same place – Mainpuri, a district town in Uttar Pradesh. Their houses were very close to each other's. They had played together as children, studied together in the same school and went to the same college. In short they were inseparable chums.

However, after finishing his MA degree, Mr Purang got married to a very decent local girl called Kunda and moved to Delhi, to take up a job in central government service. My husband also moved to Delhi – not to get a job, but to continue his studies further. He joined the Pusa Institute to do his PhD in statistics, for which he was awarded the Randhawa Gold Medal by Pandit

Jawaharlal Nehru, the then Prime Minister of India.

In those days in the 1950s most of the middle-class families in India had neither cars nor telephones in their homes, especially when they were newcomers to the capital and starting their new careers. Moreover, in India people just turn up to meet family and friends without any previous notice or information or formality. So, near the time of Diwali, we decided to go to Mr Purang's house in response to his and his wife's repeated invitations to come and stay with them for a few days. We decided to go to their place during the Dasaera vacations and just set off for their home after breakfast one fine Saturday morning, without previously informing them about the exact date and time of our reaching their place. The fact was that we ourselves were not very sure that we would really be able to go just before Diwali, and also we were not sure about the bus timings and connections to their home. Anyway, after breakfast we started at about 9.30 a.m. from Timarpur, where we used to live with my husband's sister, and after changing two or three different buses reached their home in Vinay Nagar at about 11.30 a.m.

They seemed very happy to see us and gave us a very warm welcome. We felt relaxed. Kunda Bhabi quickly prepared a delicious lunch for us. However, during the talks at lunch we gathered that on that very day there was a wedding in Kunda Bhabi's family in Ghaziabad. They had intended to go there to attend that, but since we were there now they were going to forget about it. This did not seem right to us. Both of us insisted that they should go and not cancel their plan because of us. After all, we were in Delhi only– we would come some other time. But they would not listen. It took a lot of persuasion from us to make them go to attend the family wedding.

They agreed only on one condition, and that was that we should not go back to our home in Timarpur but stay in their home. It was a matter of just one night. They would be back the next day as early as possible. We thought over the idea and agreed, thinking that we could meet so many other friends, also in New Delhi, in addition to doing our Diwali shopping. So, that was settled.

In those days we used to live with my husband's elder sister in Timarpur, a far-off colony of old Delhi, and Mr Purang lived in one of the newest colonies of New Delhi called Vinay Nagar. He lived on the first floor in a government apartment allotted to him by his office. It was not a very big house, but had two moderately sized bedrooms. At that time he did not have any children so he always had a spare bedroom for any guests. Mr Purang carried our things to this room while his wife quickly finished her packing, which had been left halfway because of our unexpected arrival.

Before they left, Mr Purang handed over the keys of his house to us and made sure that we would not give him the slip and go elsewhere to sleep. Assuring us that they would be back as early as possible the next day, they left in a hurry to catch the four-o'clock train.

Soon after they left for the station, we went out to meet other friends in New Delhi.

It was nearing 10 p.m. when we returned to our host's house. We were offered tea and snacks at every friend's house that we visited with the result that we had no room left for dinner when we returned to Mr Purang's house. So there was no need to go to the kitchen except to get some drinking water, which I did and locked the kitchen for the night. It took us another half an hour or so to change and make our bed and put away our things properly. By about 11 p.m. we were sound asleep.

Soon after midnight we were suddenly woken up by strange noises in the veranda right outside the two bedrooms. For a few minutes we tried to ignore the sounds, thinking they must be from some neighbours. We were really a bit too tired to bother and were also slightly apprehensive about opening the door in the dark to investigate. So we tried to ignore the strange sounds and went back to sleep.

We had hardly dozed off when again the sounds woke us up. This time it was not just a muffled noise but the clear sound of a key being inserted into the lock of our host's bedroom and the latch being cautiously moved. We sat upright in our bed and intently tried to listen for the sounds again. Somebody had definitely unlocked the door and was now slowly moving the latch up and down to take it out of its catch in the wall. We felt sure that thieves had entered the house through the open veranda at the back, in front of the two bedrooms, and now they were trying to open the door of our host's bedroom. We could ignore it no longer. How could we allow our friend's house to be burgled when we were there? My husband got up with a jerk, turned on the light, undid the upright bolt of our bedroom door and went out into the veranda to catch the thieves and shout for help. (There were no telephones in those days in young middle-class families!)

I had followed my husband and was right behind him, but to our great surprise when we turned on the light we couldn't see any one there at all. There was absolutely no sound or sign of anybody being there. We looked all around inside and outside the house. We thought maybe the thieves had run away, so we looked on the road, from the veranda, to see if anybody was running away. There was no one at all. Moreover, the latch and the lock were absolutely intact. There was no trace of anybody meddling with them in any way.

Assuring ourselves that the sounds must have been in our imagination only or at some neighbours, we went back to bed again. We thought that maybe because we were in a strange place in an unfamiliar environment on our own for the first time at night we were having this strange uneasy feeling of somebody intruding into the house. Thinking so, we dismissed all those disturbing sounds from our minds and tried to sleep again.

We had hardly been asleep for just a little while when again the same sort of noises disturbed our sleep. Again we got up, turned on the light and went out into the veranda. Again to our great surprise, there was absolutely no one there. We were rather frustrated and a bit frightened too. We had twice gone out and checked everywhere but had found no one at all. Was the house haunted? A stray thought came to my mind – such thoughts sometimes crop up when you hear strange sounds in the dark in a new place. We were not used to the normal hum of life in those newly built houses and thought we were unduly worrying ourselves for nothing. Thus dispersing the whole thing out of our minds we lay down again and tried to get some sleep. It was nearing 3 a.m. by this time. We were so tired and so sleepy – how we wished we could get some rest and sleep!

But sleep was slow to come. We shut our eyes and tried hard to forget about those noises, of unlocking of the door and the lifting of the latch, etc. With great difficulty in the early hours of the morning at last we were in the sweet lap of sleep, but soon the horrible noises started again. This time, however, the sound was not that of unlocking of the door or of moving the latch, but it was of things being moved around in our host's room. We could distinctly hear the sound of boxes being pushed and taken down from the stone shelf, which was built into the wall of our host's bedroom. We both got up with a jerk, but this time instead of turning on the light and going out, we slowly and cautiously went in the dark to the door adjoining the two bedrooms. We undid the bolt very, very quietly with great caution so as not to disturb the thieves but catch them red-handed.

My husband fumbled in the dark for the light switch in our host's room and found it just by the door frame. With utmost quiet and caution we switched the light on. As the sudden brightness flooded the room my husband saw some strange animal, like a sort of big cat, that jumped from the built in stone shelf to the ventilator and out. By the time I could look, the big cat, or whatever it was, had all escaped except for its thick greyish-black bushy tail, slipping out of the open slit in the ventilator above the door. It was out of the question to peep out from the high up ventilator, but to make sure that whatever it was did not drop in again, we quickly shut the ventilator tight and came back to our room to try to get some sleep.

Had that silly cat been disturbing our sleep all night? But how could a cat ever open a latch or a lock – which was the very distinct sound that we had heard initially? Also, how could it have been moving boxes around and putting them down on the floor? It was an extremely mysterious situation – completely unexplainable. Feeling a bit creepy, lying down on the bed, we were just contemplating over the whole mystery. All the sounds seemed so real, but there was no man or thief around that we could see. The only thing that we saw was that strange animal.

We indeed had a very disturbed, frustrating and frightening night. We had had practically no sleep all night. By now it was already the wee hours of the early morning, so there was no point in trying to fall asleep again. Anyway, whatever effort we might have put in to get some sleep was disturbed by the milkman ringing the bell to get that morning's supply of fresh milk. Sleepily my husband opened the kitchen door; he was hit by something in the dark but managed to fetch a pan and got the milk.

I had already started having a big headache by then and badly wanted a hot cup of tea. Now that the fresh milk was there the urge for it intensified, but I did not have the guts to enter the kitchen alone, so we both went and switched the kitchen light on. Horrors! What a hell! Unbelievable! Bowls and plates and ladles were scattered all over and tins of groceries lay upside down. Lentils and rice and spices and vegetables were strewn all over the kitchen floor. It was a scene of utter chaos, as if a bomb had just exploded there. I trembled with fear. My husband was no better.

It was vividly clear now that the voices and noises we had heard were not just in our imaginations. They were a reality. But who could have done it? We had got up thrice and checked everywhere, but never saw anybody at all. All locks, latches and everything else were perfectly intact. But surely somebody must have sneaked in to create all that havoc. Who could it be?

Certainly not that strange cat or whatever that animal was with that big bushy tail! Anyway, we saw it in the bedroom not in the kitchen. Then who had been in the kitchen? Was it the same monster which, having done enough in the kitchen, had then tried his hand in the bedroom? But how did it enter into those rooms? All locks and latches were absolutely intact. How did it sneak in? How did it manage to escape through a tiny slit in the ventilator? The house was riddled with puzzles. We could not stop wondering over the night's incredible happenings. Above all was the worry as to what our hosts would think of us. We could not look after their house even for one night!

We were feeling totally helpless and terrified. Whatever courage we had gathered in the night was slipping away now. However, things had to be put straight before our friends came back. With great courage and patience we started putting the things back as best we could.

Just then the doorbell rang again. We were petrified. Had our hosts really returned that early? Fortunately for us it was only their maidservant who had come to do the cleaning and yesterday's dishes. When she saw the state of the kitchen, she started mumbling – not directly at us, but indirectly, hinting how very clumsy we were to have created such a mess. I had to calm her down and told her that the mess was a total mystery to us as well. We had done no cooking the previous night – in fact, we had not even entered the kitchen until just a little while before she came. Listening to me she made a funny face.

"Oh, Bibiji, it must be those evil spirits, then. They really are a terrible lot. They create havoc wherever they go."

I listened to her with little interest, because maidservants of that type are the greatest gossipmongers of all.

She went on muttering, but all the same gave me a hand in putting things back. Definitely she knew better than me where to put all the different things in their proper places. After tiding up the kitchen she left because there were no dishes to be done. Having been kept awake with all those terrible things happening all night I had developed a very bad headache.

By the time she left my headache was tearing me apart. A hot cup of tea was badly needed. If things had been normal and if I had not had such a splitting headache, maybe I would have tried to light a charcoal *angithi* (an Indian charcoal stove), but after all that effort of putting things back and listening to that lady's continuous chatter, I was feeling very tired and could hardly stand or keep my eyes open. My husband was not very good at lighting those *angithis*. Perhaps he had never lit one in all his life and perhaps he did not feel like looking for the charcoal and getting his hands black with coal in the cold. What were we to do? We both needed some tea badly. We were just thinking when suddenly my husband's eyes fell on a kerosene oil stove on one of the side shelves. With delight he lugged at it, brought it down and lighted it up skilfully. He was actually quite an expert at lighting those kerosene oil stoves. All through his student life in hostels he had used them regularly to heat up milk. Elated he made nice hot cups of tea for both of us. Fortunately by putting things back in their places in the kitchen we knew exactly where the tea leaves and sugar were.

When my headache was slightly better we got ready and started packing up our things, to be able to leave as soon as our hosts returned. I did not want to stay in that weird house even for a minute more than absolutely necessary. Actually we both wanted to rush back to our own home in Timarpur but there was no way we could have left because the keys of the house were with us. Anyway, it would have been extremely discourteous to leave the house without taking leave of our hosts. Willy-nilly we had to stay there till they came back. We knew for sure that it would be difficult for them to come back before evening teatime at the earliest, although they had said that they would be home definitely by lunchtime. How I wished there was a phone around! But that was only a wishful thinking. Telephones were a rare luxury in those days. There was no way of contacting our friends. We had no choice but to wait till they would come back.

After the night's terrible experience, we were sort of disenchanted and felt rather ill at ease and totally disinclined to do anything – even to have breakfast. We just needed to be out of the house.

So we decided to go to see the nearby local market. As I have already stated, it was near the time of Diwali and we had gone to Mr Purang's place thinking that while we were there we would do our Diwali shopping as well from the New Delhi market.

Connaught Place had the best shops and the latest designs in those days. Karol Bagh was also gaining reputation for its big beautiful shops.

Our friends had told us that they would be back as soon as possible, but we knew well that they would not be back before lunch at the earliest. With the shopping list in mind and hoping to find at least some of the things in the Vinay Nagar market, we proceeded towards those new shops. We also needed to have something to eat, and to bring some cooked food back for our hosts, in case they turned up before lunch. I had no intention or inclination to cook anything in their haunted kitchen.

We were so much put off by the previous night's strange experiences that we could not concentrate even on shopping. The Vinay Nagar market was quite small anyway and the things we had in mind were also not available there. We had a quick round of the shops and came back after taking brunch in a small café. The food was very good, fresh and tasty with a distinct hot Panjabi flavour. We ate heartily, combining breakfast and lunch together, got some *chola bhatura* packed for our hosts and returned back to their home.

By the time we reached their home it was nearly two o'clock in the afternoon. Our hosts had not yet come back. We did not really expect them back till four or five in the evening, so we just tried to relax in their sitting room. I did not want to go into that bedroom again. Waiting was a long moment. The more anxiously we waited the more delayed they seemed to get. At long last we heard the sound of a scooter rickshaw stopping in front of the house. They were home at last!

The two friends had a hearty hug. Kunda Bhabi went on apologising for leaving us on our own on our very first stay with them. She is a very sweet lady and I was very happy to see her again.

After the heartfelt greetings, she asked us if we had a comfortable stay in their house in their absence and whether we had any difficulty in finding out things for cooking, etc. We did not have the courage to tell her what had been happening all night. Still it had to be told but we did not know where and how to start. Seeing our drawn faces, she got a bit concerned.

"Why, you seem to be hiding something from us? Weren't

you comfortable? Did you feel cold? Did you have a meal last night and this morning? I hope you did not have difficulty in finding out things?"

Mr Purang was also looking at us with a question mark on his face.

Suddenly Kunda Bhabi remembered something and went to our room and saw our things all packed up. She came back startled and asked in astonishment why we had packed up our suitcases.

After a little hesitation we had to tell the truth.

"Oh," she said, "you didn't see the ghost, did you? I am so very sorry – I quite forgot to tell you about that."

"About what?" we both exclaimed in alarm.

"About the ghost that visits the house."

"A real ghost?" I asked, terrified.

"Yes," she answered matter-of-factly, as if it was the most normal, natural thing to be.

My husband and I were totally taken aback. We only hear stories about ghosts; we don't expect to see them. But Kunda Bhabi was talking about this ghost as easily as if she was talking about a family member.

"What? Do you have ghosts living in the house?" I asked, mystified.

"No, he does not live here, but comes every now and then to eat some sugar." She continued: "He is only a poor little thing perhaps a diabetic who died craving for sugar in his youth. He does not do any harm to us or to anything else in the house. He just eats two or three scoops of sugar every time he comes, and then he goes away quietly. As a matter of fact, he protects our house from other evil spirits."

This was hard to believe after our night's experience.

"What do you mean – a real ghost visiting you every now and then? And how – in what way – does he protect your house?" I asked, bewildered.

"He keeps other evil spirits away from our house," she replied calmly.

This was all beyond our wildest imagination.

Then addressing my husband, Mr Purang himself said, "You know, Purushottam, ghosts are indeed a reality in this colony."

"How come you never ever before mentioned about them to me?" interrupted my husband.

"Because I was afraid that you would not believe me in the first place; and secondly, if I told you, what would you think of me – a coward? I was too scared to talk about them because I feared that if I mentioned them to anybody, they would take revenge on me as they have on some others. You know, there have been instances here with fatal consequences when people talked about them or ignored their warnings."

"Oh, really? Do they come and kill? Unbelievable! But you say they give a warning before killing how do they warn you? How? In what way?" asked my husband.

"Yes, they do."

"In what way?"

"You know, Puroshottam, when we first came here, Mummy and Yash (Purang Sahib's younger brother) came to visit us during Yash's summer vacations. We used to sleep on the roof under the open sky. There was no toilet on the roof, so when Yash needed to go to the bathroom at night we just asked him to use the drain, made for rainwater to flow down. No sooner he had used it, a heavy voice shouted from the alleyway below, "How dare you make my place filthy! Never ever do that again."

We thought it must be some neighbour passing by, so we did not pay much attention to it; but when Yash tried to use the drain again, the same voice was heard again saying, "I warned you never to urinate here. I am not going to spare you now. I am coming to fetch you."

Yash was terrified and shrieked with fright. We all heard his shriek and got up. I quickly switched the light on, and saw Yash shaking.

He shouted, "Save me! Save me! Don't let him take me away!"

I held him steady and asked, "Why Yash, who is taking you away? Why are you so frightened?"

"The ghost! The ghost!" he just about managed to say before he fainted.

Yash suffered such a shock that it took him months to recover from it.

After this incident, we decided to leave this colony. We searched for a house in many different localities but could not find accommodation which we could afford, so we had no other choice but to stay in this government-allotted house only and put up with the frightening things. After all, we are not the only ones to be afflicted by them – there are thousands of others living in this colony who are in the same position.

"What do you mean 'put up' with them?" asked my husband.

"Now we don't ignore any warnings or threats given by them. We have learnt to take them seriously and let them do what they want to do."

"This is a serious matter. Why, for God's sake, has nobody reported the matter to the government?" my husband asked infuriated.

"Yes! Purushottam, many people did complain to the government, but everyone got the same reply. We were told that after partition, when the government was suddenly faced with the problem of accommodating an influx of refugees from Pakistan, it had no choice but to expand the perimeters of Delhi and build new houses. The nearest and easiest was this area which, we were told, was originally a vast expanse of graves, both ancient and recent. Some of the graves were very new, but the builders dug those up too. Ever since then, the whole area has become rampant with ghosts and spirits of all sorts. People say that the spirits of those who had not yet achieved peace after death have become active again and are taking revenge on those who have come to live here."

We remained silent for some time, but eventually I could not help asking as to why they thought that the ghost visiting them was a harmless one and how did they make friends with him?

Kunda Bhabi replied, "You know, when we first set up our kitchen and brought the rations in (everything was rationed in those days, and sugar was a particularly scarce commodity) we soon realised that someone was helping himself to our ration of sugar. At first I thought it must be the maidservants stealing sugar from the larder, but they both swore that they had not taken away even one spoonful of sugar. I believed them but started keeping the sugar tin hidden behind the bigger containers of rice, wheat, lentils, etc. Still I noticed that scoops of sugar were going missing. I asked everybody in the house if they had noticed any stranger going into the kitchen, but nobody had seen anyone. We started falling short of sugar every week. It was extremely costly and difficult to buy sugar in the black market, so we started putting the sugar under lock and key in a special container. However, to my horror, sugar was still going missing – two or three scoops every second or third night. I was by then more terrified than mystified."

Kunda Bhabi talked it over with her husband, his family and her friends. Her friends from outside Vinay Nagar Colony suggested that they must do some kind of spiritual ritual to get rid of those evil spirits. They had heard of stories similar to Kunda Bhabhi's in other houses also and felt sure that it could be only the wandering spirits who were terrorizing people and creating havoc wherever they went. It must be one of those ghosts helping himself of their sugar. Incredible though it sounded, but there was no other explanation either.

Kunda Bhabi's mother-in-law suggested that she should get some special prayers and *havan* done by a holy person who specialises in warding off evil spirits, and that she should give some donations to charities. Maybe if she helped other people, God would help her to get rid of their sugar thief. Kunda Bhabi tried everything that anybody suggested, but nothing worked.

In the end she gave up. She had nothing else in her power except to pray to the invisible thing not to harm them in any other way and to confine his mischief to the sugar container only. After that she stopped having nightmares. In general she and Mr Purang both felt much more at ease than they had ever been before in that house.

Kunda Bhabi said, "Now we have made friends with him. We do not say anything to him and he does not do any harm to us.

After our night's experience, I was not quite prepared to believe that. I asked her, "If he is friendly, then why did he create such havoc last night? Apart from robbing us of our sleep, he was a continuous nuisance and a fright all night."

Kunda Bhabi thought over it for a little while then said, "Maybe you disturbed him in his nightly helping of sugar from our kitchen. Maybe he was frightened and returned back with his friends to vent his anger. If he had not been friendly, he could have frightened you out of your wits, as some of them do – like the one which threatened Yash. I feel sure that it was not our ghost but his friends who created all that havoc in the kitchen."

We both looked at her in sheer astonishment.

She said, "If you don't believe me, you can watch him come tonight and see for yourself that, apart from the sugar tin, he does not touch anything else."

"No, no," we said, "we have had enough of him. We have no desire to see him in person. Actually we would like to take leave of you now, if you don't mind."

Hearing this, Purang Saheb jumped up from his seat, as if something has suddenly bitten him. He appeared to be dumbfounded. After a while when he regained his composure, and asked angrily, "How could you ever think of such a thing? Do you think I will let you go like this? No, dear friend, no, you are not going anywhere. With great difficulty we managed to persuade you and Bhabiji to come. At long last when we are together you are thinking of abandoning us. No way! You are not going anywhere."

We tried all our tactics and made many excuses, but no arguments prevailed on him. Mr Purang refused to listen to anything. All our efforts to take our leave of them failed. We were left with no choice but to do as he wished.

Kunda Bhabi seemed elated. Happiness seemed to be bursting out of her, as if she had won a great battle. "Now I will be able to show you our nightly visitor. You have got to see him, otherwise I know you will never again come back to see us."

I must admit that there was some truth in her assertion. I had decided never again to go to that haunted house. But their love prevailed over everything else.

With triumph she said, "Tonight I am going to put the lock on the sugar canister in front of you. I will lock the kitchen door and give the keys to you to keep for the night."

I was really frightened by her statement. Respectfully I told her not to do any such thing. If she wanted to lock the sugar tin and the kitchen door, she was welcome to do so, but I refused to keep the keys with me. They both had a hearty laugh at my statement. Cracking jokes, laughing and talking over several cups of tea and coffee, we lost track of time. Soon it was time for dinner. Kunda Bhabi quickly prepared some hot rice *pullao* and we already had some *chola bhatura* which we had brought for them from the bazaar. Dinner tasted doubly delicious in their joyous company.

The ghosts and our last night's ordeal had gone into the recesses of our memories, but at bedtime the creepy feeling took over me again. I wished we had gone back! My husband tried to console me as best he could. I knew though, that he himself was not feeling very comfortable either. However, there was nothing that we could do. He kept on telling me to close my eyes and try to sleep. I tried hard to do that but with no result.

In spite of my best efforts, involuntarily my eyes were focused on the little slit between the door and its frame. Sleep was nowhere near me. Then, at about midnight, I saw an apparition in the veranda. There was enough light from the street light to see that it was not what we would normally visualise as a ghost. The form had no arms or legs or head covered in white. It was just an oblong apparition of greyish mist and vapour. I felt too thrilled to be afraid. It wasn't a frightening thing at all. I opened my eyes even wider and listened intently for any sound. The misty formation moved out of sight as it approached the kitchen door. I was very curious to see its movements so I silently got up from the bed and, without switching on the light, went and stood closer to the crevice and saw the figure disappear through the kitchen door.

Curiously I waited, but I did not see him come out. Perhaps he had felt my presence and slipped out through the kitchen window. Now that the ghost had gone, I returned to bed and fell sound asleep.

We were woken up next morning by Kunda Bhabi knocking at the door and asking for the key to the kitchen door. Oh, my God! had she really left the key under our pillow?

I sprang to my feet and opened the door for her. There she was standing smiling.

"Good morning," we both said to each other.

Then I asked her in surprise, "Bhabiji, did you really leave the key under our pillow?"

She grinned and said, "How could I, when you had specifically asked me not to? I left it on the mantelpiece, behind a picture. Look, here it is. Now come with me."

Holding my hand, she took me to the kitchen, unlocked the

door, lifted the latch and entered the kitchen. Then she unlocked the sugar tin.

"See," she said triumphantly, "isn't it exactly as I had told you?"

I could clearly see the hollows where the sugar had been scooped out.

This was amazing indeed. A real ghost visiting a real house! I had seen him and his doings with my own eyes.

Fortunately this encounter was nothing like as frightening as my first encounter with a ghost was. That took place when I was in my high school, where one of the basements was said to be inhabited by evil spirits. There were scratches made by their fingernails on the dirty, dusty ventilator pans, which were later replaced by solid wood panels.

The bushy greyish-black tail of the monster that I saw slipping through the slit in the ventilator of our friends' house has remained a mystery. Perhaps that was another ghost looking for woollen clothing for the approaching winter.

Sometimes I wonder, now, with the population explosion everywhere in India, each colony bursting out of its boundaries, with buzzing horns and crushing crowds, if those poor ghosts or spirits had any chance of survival! I am sure there are no bushy tails or ghostly sugar-eaters any more in Vinay Nagar. The present-day noise and hustle-bustle of Delhi must have frightened them away. Spirits have no chance of survival amidst the crowds and noises of those heavily populated colonies now.

NB: This is a personal experience of the writer in the year 1951.

THE PICTURE

It was the summer of 1972 and the first day of our visit to India from Britain. In those days we used to go and stay with our elder sister, Radhe Rani, in Daryaganj, Delhi. Jiji, Jijaji and their children all used to live in the big family home built by Jijaji's father. Theirs was an extended joint family; not only did they stay with their parents but also all the rest of Jijaji's married and unmarried brothers and sisters all lived in the same big house together. We were accommodated along with the rest of the family in their big family home. Every member of the household used to greet us very warmly.

That time was no exception. After a very warm welcome, a lavish dinner and much gossiping, it was at last time for bed. Jijaji took out the charpoys (the Indian light beds which can easily be stored away when not in use) on the open roof in front of their bedroom on the first floor. Jijaji and my niece, Sushma, made the beds for us, spreading the cotton rugs (*daries*) and the freshly laundered, white cleaned and ironed sheets over them, with pillows for all the beds with clean white pillowcases on them. It was well past midnight when we all finally settled to sleep.

The nights are rather short in India during summer months. The morning sun is out by 4.45 or 5 a.m., and it is broad daylight by six o'clock. By the time I got up, Jiji and Jijaji were already up and busy with their morning routine. I was woken up only when the gentle rays of the morning sun started spreading their glare on my sleepy eyes and face. Feeling a bit embarrassed for getting up so late, I headed straight for the toilets situated across the open roof, opposite Jiji and Jijaji's room. When I came out into the wash-hand-basin area (which was outside between the two toilets), and when I had finished washing my hands I saw Sushma standing by my bed, holding a silky paper in her hands. Somehow, even from that distance, and without anybody saying anything to me, I had a gut feeling of what it was. Still, with some curiosity I walked up to my bed.

When my niece saw me, she showed me the silky paper she was holding in her hands and asked, "Mausi, do you always sleep with this picture under your pillow?"

"What picture? I never sleep with any picture under my pillow."

"Then what is this?" she enquired, showing me the paper she was holding in her hand. She said, "Look – I found it under your pillow when I came to fold away your bedding."

"Under my pillow?"

"Yes," and she handed over the silky paper to me.

To my utter astonishment, it really was a picture, on smooth, silky paper, of the Divine Mother, Ma Durga riding majestically on her lion. I could not believe my eyes. How on earth did a picture of Ma appear under my pillow? Surely, my sister must have left it there when she made the beds for us at night.

My niece and I took the picture inside the room to ask Jiji if she had put that picture under my pillow.

Jiji was as surprised to see it as I was. She had certainly not put it under my pillow – she had never even seen it before.

She showed the picture to Jijaji and asked if he knew anything about it.

Jijaji looked at the picture in astonishment and said that he knew nothing about it and, like Jiji, he too had never seen that particular picture before.

We were all wondering about it.

Then Jiji thought for a moment and said, "Maybe it is my mother-in-law's. I will go down and ask her."

She took the picture downstairs and asked her mother-in-law if the picture belonged to her.

She too looked at it with sheer astonishment and exclaimed, "What a big and beautiful picture of the Divine Mother it is! It looks so fresh and so nice. There are no creases or fold marks," she said with great admiration and reverence. But certainly it did not belong to her.

By then all the rest of the family had gathered around and were admiring the beautiful picture. Surprisingly, none of them had ever seen it before. It was a big, beautiful coloured picture of the Divine Mother, Goddess Ma Durga, about ten by eight inches and absolutely intact. "Where did you find it?" they asked my niece.

"I found it under Mausi's pillow."

"Oh, really?"

But how did it appear, and from where? Under my pillow! It was not such a windy or stormy night that the picture could have blown over from some neighbour's house. It was a very quiet, starry, windless, close night. Even if it had blown over, it would have been on top of things not under a pillow! How did it happen? How did an inanimate object manage to get itself under a pillow?

Nobody could explain the appearance of the Divine Mother's picture under my pillow, then or even now. It looked as if it had come to me mysteriously, nobody knows from where. Indeed the Almighty's ways are strange!

My sister's mother-in-law told aloud to all, "Since the picture was found under Sushilaji's pillow, it must be given to her." Then she looked at me and instructed me to look after the picture well and said that I must always keep it with me and treat it with reverence and care.

Since that day the beautiful picture of Mother Goddess is with me, but the mystery of its appearance has remained unsolved.

I can't say that the appearance of the Divine Mother's picture opened up the floodgates of heaven for us. No, nothing like that happened. This much, however, I will say: that ever since the advent of the picture, the great tensions and unrest in our family, due to some intrigues by jealous colleagues who created misunderstanding between my husband and the management of the institute where he was working, were cleared up for ever. The picture brought peace, happiness and harmony once again to our lives.

We had moved to Britain for good and led a much happier and fulfilling life than at that time in India. The hitherto troubling worries were all over. Thanks a million to the Divine Mother who left us a symbol of her divine grace to take us out of those troubled times.

The enigmatic picture is still with me in our house in my household shrine. Though much faded and somewhat time-worn by now, it is still a reminder of the Divine Grace which came when it was much needed in our family. Actually it is a source of even greater strength to me in my lonely life now.

DIAMONDS ARE NOT FOR EVER

Since my childhood I have always been hearing that 'diamonds are for ever'. Somehow I had begun to believe this popular saying, but soon after my marriage I faced two instances which contradicted the old belief. I can say with surety now that diamonds are *not* for ever, as you can read in the following two instances.

EPISODE 1

"Aren't you lucky? What a lot of jewellery! Look at this!" a friend of mine said, looking enviously at the solitaire diamond nose stud, which was still in its tiny case on top of the other jewellery boxes.

"Oh, what a big diamond!"

"The most beautiful nose ring I have ever seen."

"It must be very costly."

"They are rich people, you know. I had only heard about them before, but now I can see it for myself."

Such were some of the comments that reached my ears from my cousins and friends who were all anxiously awaiting my return from the Janwasa (a temporary residence arranged by the bride's family for the groom's family to stay if they were coming from another city). They were all very eager to see all the gifts, including jewellery and clothes that my in-laws were expected to give me.

As I heard their comments, I took a glance at their faces. Some had real appreciation and contentment on my good fortune; but I could feel the tinge of envy in some eyes.

Indeed my nose ring was very beautiful, with a big diamond studded in beautiful tiny delicate petals of gold around it, like a jewel in a flower. But, alas! my nose was not pierced, so it was no use to me. My sisters-in-law suggested that if I want they could get a finger ring made for me from the diamond in the nose stud.

'That would be nice,' I thought, and I gave the nose ring to them so that the diamond in it could be fixed into a finger ring.

Having left the solitaire diamond stud with them, I travelled to Pune with my husband and quite forgot about it.

A few years later when I returned back to Delhi from Pune, I remembered my diamond nose stud, and thought it must have been converted into a finger ring by then. I was silently expecting that my sister-in-law, with whom I had left it, would take it out herself and hand it over to me. Inwardly I was quite excited that soon I would have a beautiful solitaire diamond ring. Two or three days passed by, but there was no mention of the ring at all. Then one day, hesitantly, I enquired about it myself.

My sister-in-law looked at me with a sort of blank face as if to say it would have been better if I had not asked about it. Her usual cheerful expression immediately changed to one of worry and helplessness. I could guess something was wrong, but I could never imagine what.

"Oh yes, your nose ring! Yes, it was with me," she muttered as if very painfully.

I looked at her. Why had she turned so pale? I tried to read her face, but apart from worry I could read nothing else.

To put her at ease, I said, "Don't worry if it is not convenient for you at this moment. You can take it out later."

She nodded her head and said, "It is not a question of convenience, but I do not know how to tell you."

"Why, what has happened?" I enquired politely.

"I am so sorry, Bahuji [the word for a daughter-in-law or a younger relative's wife] but your diamond nose ring is no longer with me," my sister-in-law said with a grim face.

"What? Where is it then?" I enquired with a little anxiety.

"I do not know, but alas! it is not with me any more," she replied solemnly.

I looked at her, not quite knowing what to say.

After a little while she gathered up courage and said: "I do not know how to tell you, but it is not with me any more." After a little pause she added, "Yes, I am so sorry, but it seems to have disappeared miraculously. Somebody has made away with it."

"What?" I asked in disbelief. "Was there a burglary in the house?"

"No, there was no burglary as such, but something similar happened."

"Why, what happened, then?" I was quite surprised – no burglary, but a precious thing had been stolen. "How did it happen?" I asked.

"You know, Bahuji," continued my sister-in-law apologetically, "after you left for Pune we thought there was no urgency to get the ring made immediately, so we put it in the family safe, thinking that we shall get the ring made nearer the time when you will be coming back to Delhi. Now, when we heard that you are coming I took it out of the safe to take it to the jeweller's. A friend of mine from our block of flats had been asking me to accompany her to the jeweller's for a long time but for one reason or another I was not able to go with her, so I thought I better take her now with me if she wanted. On inquiring from her, she was more than happy to come with me.

"She did come happily, but along with her came a bunch of other ladies as well. Although they all lived in the same block of flats as ours, but except saying hello once in a while, I did not know them so well personally. Seeing them all just when we were about to go out was a bit awkward. I looked at my friend enquiringly, wondering why she had brought all the neighbourhood with her. It looked as though going to the jeweller's was a thing of great excitement for all of them. I had not expected my friend to broadcast it to all her neighbours, and I was a bit upset about it, but there they were – all six or seven of them. I did not know how to turn them away! I decided that I would neither take your diamond stud out nor go to the jewellers that day, and I told my friend so."

'But I want to go,' she insisted. 'I have got some urgent work at the jeweller's and that is why I had been requesting you to accompany me for so long, but you have just been postponing it. Now when I have come all prepared, suddenly you decide not to go.'

"What could I say? I tried to make an excuse and told her that I had just remembered some other more urgent work and wouldn't be able to go with her that day.

"She perhaps guessed rightly why I didn't really want to go and said aloud, 'Don't be afraid of them. They are all friends from our building.' She continued: 'They have come just to have a look at that solitaire diamond stud. Please show it to them now.'

"I thought, 'That was exactly what I did not want to do.' I was in a very awkward position. I really did not want to show the diamond to all those ladies, but could find no way out. Willy nilly, in the end I had to take it out.

"Out of sheer curiosity they all tried to grab it from me all at once. All of them wanted to have a look at it at the same time. They seemed to be more than anxious to hold it in their hands than just to have a look at it. It passed from hand to hand with exclamations about its beauty and estimates of its cost.

"After a while I told my friend, 'We are getting late. Let's go.'

"She agreed and asked the ladies to give her back the nose ring. But, but where was it? All the ladies denied one by one having possession of it saying, 'I had passed it to her and I had passed it to her.'

"Perhaps the one who had stolen it had already slipped away from the group. I asked the ladies again and again, but they all denied having possession of it. We searched for it all around the room, behind and under the furniture, in every nook and corner, but there was no trace of it. I didn't know which one had taken it. I certainly could not ask them to undress so that I could look for it under their garments. I grew impatient and lost my temper, but my shouting and nervousness had no effect on them. They all pretended to be absolutely innocent, but among all those hers the nose ring had simply vanished, disappeared without a trace, as if it had been dissolved into thin air. Nobody confessed having possession of it.

"I pleaded hard with them but to no avail. Who had stolen it I could not say, but somebody has definitely made away with it. Oh, God! What am I going to do now? I didn't know how I was ever going to tell you. I could not think what to do. My head was reeling with anxiety and fear. I felt I would never be able to show my face to you again. Sick with worry, I decided to call the police.

"Just then the doorbell rang. It was the children come back from school. I did not want to create a scene in front of the children."

I listened to my sister-in-law's narration silently, not knowing exactly what to say.

She continued: "Finding the door open, the ladies started slipping away one by one. Last of all the lady who I thought was a friend came to me and tried to reassure me: "Don't worry, I will surely find out the culprit and report her to the police.

"So saying, she also left. I sincerely thought she would help me to trace the culprit. After all, it was she who had brought all of those ladies in. I waited for her for many days, but so far she has not shown her face again.

"With the children back from school, I had to look after them. So the matter was hushed away at that time, but it has been nagging at the back of my head ever since."

I was quite disturbed to hear all this and also a bit sad to lose such a precious thing, but at the same time I felt great sympathy for my honest and innocent sister-in-law. I tried to reassure her myself, telling her not to worry. "If it is gone, it is gone. There's no use brooding over it now."

My sister-in-law was difficult to comfort. She was very upset and worried even after so many days.

"You know, Bahuji," she continued, "I still regret not reporting the matter to the police then and there, but whom would I report? I could not say with certainty which amongst them all was the actual thief. Convicting them all would be unjust, but I was very angry with the lady who I considered to be my friend, and I am very angry with myself as well. Why did I have to take the diamond stud out at all? I should have been more firm and refused to take it out. But how could I have known that there were thieves living in our own building? Really you can't trust anybody these days."

I tried to console my sister-in-law again, but she was too upset to be consoled easily.

She seemed to be full of remorse. She said, "Sorry, Bahuji. Father had kept that solitaire diamond for you with such love and care and was very happy to pass it on to you, but just because of my carelessness the precious family heirloom is lost. I feel so bad about it."

Even I felt very bad when I realised that it was an heirloom kept by my mother-in-law for me, and that she herself had got it from her mother-in-law. But what could I do now? I just remembered the old saying: 'It's no use crying over spilt milk.'

I had full trust and confidence in my sister-in-law. She was an extremely simple, very caring and a very loving lady who doted on my husband, perhaps because she had no son of her own. Ladies just took advantage of her simplicity.

Whatever may have happened but the precious family heirloom, the beautiful solitaire diamond, had gone – gone for ever.

This was the first experience that taught me that diamonds are *not* for ever.

Episode 2

"Mummyji, I have been thinking about it for a long time but have been a bit hesitant. Now that your programme of going to India has been finalised I wonder if I could ask you a favour?" asked Shyama, my daughter-in-law.

"Yes, dear. Do you want something from India?"

"No Mummyji, I don't need anything. It's just that Rakesh has finished his medical. Soon his internship will be over and as soon as he settles in his job I would like to get him married."

"Yes, I am also eagerly waiting for that auspicious day."

"So, Mummyji, I was thinking – you remember the old emerald and diamond set you gave me at my marriage?"

"Yes, the same that was given to me by Maji at my marriage? That is a precious heirloom and I want it to remain in our family always. I hope you have it safe with you and have looked after it well?"

"Yes, Mummyji. You told me so when you gave it to me. It is only that after all these years of use the shine is not quite as it used to be – besides, it needs some repairs too. I was wondering if you could please take it with you to India and get it repaired and polished at your cousin's shop? It would be then ready to give it to our daughter-in-law when the time comes."

"That is a good idea. I don't think there would be any problem in getting the work done at Mohan's shop," I said with confidence.

"Thank you so much, Mummyji. I will take it out from the bank tomorrow."

Next day she brought out the set from the bank and handed it over to me to take to India with me.

On reaching Delhi the first thing I did was to contact my cousin who owns the jewellery shop. He was very excited to know that I was in India and immediately invited my sister and me for dinner the next day. I was very keen to see them as soon as possible, so accepted the invitation happily. I normally stayed with my elder sister whenever I went to Delhi.

Next day when going for dinner I took the ancestral set with me. After the usual general gossip I came to the point and showed my cousin the set that my daughter-in-law wanted repaired and polished.

He looked at it in amazement and exclaimed, "Oh, what a beautiful set! It must be very old because they don't make jewellery of this type any more. It would cost a fortune to get one made like this now."

"Yes, indeed it would," I said, "and that is exactly why I have brought it to you. I am sure in your hands and in your shop it will be safe. I don't feel confident about leaving it at just any jeweller. Shyama comes to India every year but she was a bit hesitant about asking a favour from you, so I have brought it for her.

"Why does she feel hesitant with me? You must have been telling her some frightening stories about me," said my cousin naughtily. "I appreciate your confidence in me, but why do you want to get it polished? It is very good as it is," said my cousin.

"I know, but the set needs some minor repairs as well. The clasp in the bracelet is broken and some of the links in the necklace are either dented or missing. I know the real value of the set is in its diamonds, not its workmanship or design, but I think we should make it wearable before we pass it on to the next generation – that is, before we give it to Rakesh's wife."

"Oh, I see. Don't worry, Jiji – just leave it to me and then you will see what wonders your cousin can do for you. I shall make it look like new."

"No! No, don't do that. It should show its ancestry."

"Don't you worry – its original beauty shall remain intact," my cousin assured me, "only I will have to sit and see the work done right under my nose. You know, if our old expert workman was here, there would have been no problem but this new man I would not trust completely. Our old trusted Mr Bakshi has gone to his village for his daughter's wedding and has taken one month off. The person working in his place is also quite trustworthy, but I do not want to take any risks with priceless jewels like this, especially as it is yours, brought all the way back from Britain."

I gave my cousin a loving pat on his shoulder and said, "That is just like you, and that is exactly why I have brought it to you."

"By the way, how long are you here?" asked my cousin.

"Oh, I am here for a full one month."

"Then there is no problem at all. Our old Mr Bakshi will be back by then and I would rather get it done by him than anyone else."

"Fine," I said with great relief. "Shyama was so worried about it."

Entrusting my old gold, diamond and emerald set to my cousin, I left light-heartedly for my sister's place.

After staying two more days with my sister, I continued my travels within India, visiting friends and relatives in Agra, Jaipur, Udaipur, Bombay and Pune. On returning back to Delhi, just two days before my return flight to Britain, I phoned my cousin about the set.

He told me that Mr Bakshi had stayed at his village a bit longer than expected, but had come back the night before and was working on the set at that very moment. He told me not to worry as he would see to it that I got my set back before my flight.

"Good," I said, and I got busy with my final shopping and packing before my flight.

Next day it was almost 8 p.m. but my set had still not arrived. I phoned my cousin. He said, "Mr Bakshi is on his way to your sister's house and should be there soon."

I was getting a bit nervous and praying that he would come sooner rather than later so that I would have enough time to pack it up properly.

It was past 11 p.m. when Mr Bakshi finally knocked at the door. I heaved a sigh of relief. Mr Bakshi handed over the set personally to me, wrapped up in an ordinary shopping bag as if it contained groceries. He was the most trusted workman of the shop, and he has been there since my uncle's time, so I did not think it necessary to check the things, but my sister's in-laws advised me to check them anyway. Actually they were all very keen to see the set once again. It was a feast for everyone's eyes. Reluctantly I took the box out of the bag and opened it.

I was amazed to see the difference myself. It was a dazzling beauty. With big ohs and ahs each individual piece – the necklace, the bracelet, the earrings and the ring – was passed from hand to hand.

Just as I was putting the pieces back in their case, the lights suddenly went off. There was a complete power failure – no lights at all anywhere! I was told that power cuts had become a regular occurrence because of a power shortage in India. In my time there had been no such power shortages and no power cuts.

I was not used to it. Along with so many other things this phenomenon was new to me.

But what was I to do now? How would I know that every piece was back in its place in the box? It was pitch dark. Hurriedly I slipped everything back into the plastic bag in which the set was brought. (I wished I had never opened the case, but my niece and her aunt very much wanted to try the necklace around their own necks.) Now it was impossible to put everything back in its place in the box in the dark.

My niece, Kamal, led me to my room with the help of a torch. I packed the things as best as I could in total darkness and went to bed. Fortunately Kamal had decided to sleep in my room that day with me. She wanted to spend as much time as possible with me before my flight.

There was not much time to sleep anyway, because my flight was at 6 a.m. We had to leave home by 3 a.m. Fortunately the light had been restored by then.

On reaching home in Britain I called Shyama to my room to hand over the set to her safely. I took out the plastic bag carefully and started taking out the pieces one by one. "Here is the necklace" I said as I handed it over to her with a little pride in my eyes. She looked at it with great admiration and thanked me. Next came out the ring and then the earrings, but where was the bracelet? Where was it? To my utter shock and distress the most exquisite piece of the set – the bracelet – was missing. I turned the whole box upside down and asked Shyama to look into the folds of all the clothes. I thought maybe it had slipped out of the bag and had fallen somewhere among the clothes. Together we searched every packet, every paper and every pocket in my purse as well as in my travel suitcase, but all in vain. It was nowhere – not in the suitcase, not in any pocket, not in any purse. Everything was searched inside out again and again and again, but to no avail.

In the end I decided to phone up my sister in Delhi, in case in the dark the bracelet had slipped out of the bag instead of inside the bag. It might have fallen in the room where we were sitting, or in the bedroom upstairs where we had slept. When I rang her up she was as much taken aback as I was. Neither she nor anyone else in the house had seen it. If they had, they would have called me themselves.

"But, you know," she said, "as soon you left both the servants left too without any warning or previous notice. It could be that they had found it while cleaning the house in the morning and picked it up and made away with it. I wondered why the servants had fled so suddenly without any notice – now this explains why."

"Have you looked in their room? They might have gone to sleep again after waking up so early for us."

"My reaction was the same," said my sister. "When they did not appear at breakfast time I sent Vijay [my nephew] to wake them up, but they had left, bag and baggage. There is no trace of them. I have made enquiries, but nobody knows anything about them. Now I feel sure that they have run away with your diamond bracelet. I am going to report them to the police."

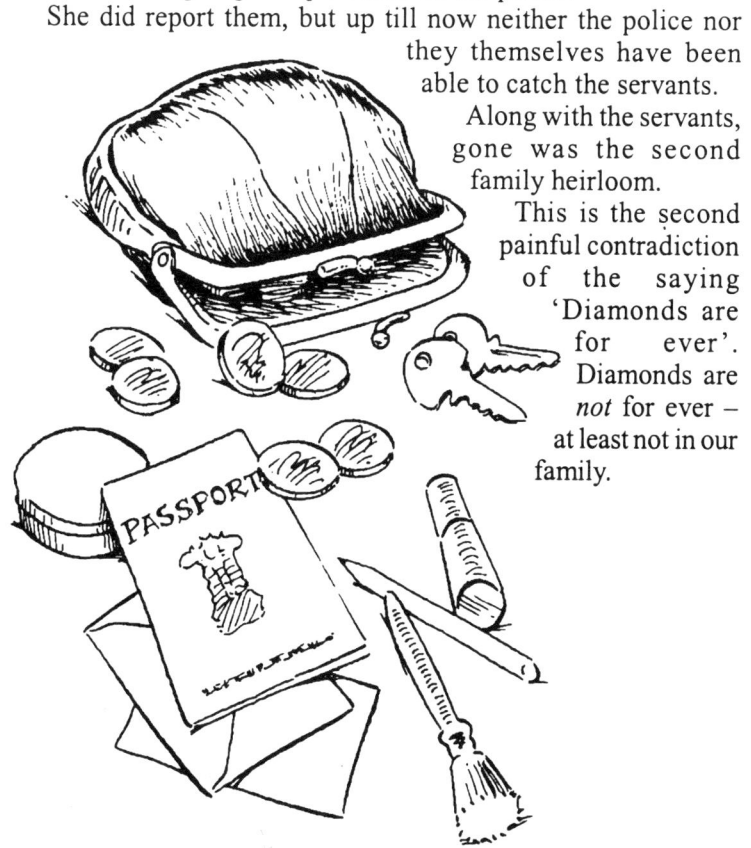

She did report them, but up till now neither the police nor they themselves have been able to catch the servants.

Along with the servants, gone was the second family heirloom.

This is the second painful contradiction of the saying 'Diamonds are for ever'. Diamonds are *not* for ever – at least not in our family.

93

THE POWER OF PRAYER OR A MIRACLE

After the following incident it has become my firm belief that prayers are heard and miracles do happen.

It was the night of Diwali, 1980. Diwali, as the world knows, is the biggest and the most important festival of all Hindus. We were staying in the UK at that time at the seaside town of Aberystwyth, some 250 miles from London. Our eldest son, Dnyanesh, was just married that year and was working with the Science Research Council at Oxford. My younger son, Rajul, was studying for his Masters degree in Manchester.

The Divine Mother, Lakshmi is worshipped on Diwali Day as the goddess of wealth and prosperity. In our homes we consider the daughters-in-law as representative of Mother Lakshmi. They are the true wealth of a family as they bring the hope of new generations. I very much wanted that our newly wed daughter-in-law, Seema, the Lakshmi of our house, should be at home for her first Diwali puja in our house. My son's job was new and it was difficult for him take any leave from his work for our big festival.

My husband said, "It does not matter. We shall celebrate Diwali on the weekend nearest to Diwali. If they can start a bit early and reach here by eight or nine on the Friday night, it should be all right. They will still be in time for puja"

He asked our son, Dnyanesh, to let us know if he could do that.

Next day he phoned us and said, "Yes."

He had taken half a day off on the Friday and hoped to start soon after lunch. We felt very happy and told him to also pick up our younger son, Rajul also from Manchester, and our youngest daughter from Warwick on his way. Our elder daughter, Shalini, had arrived earlier and was at home with us.

I would like to inform my friends from outside India – i.e. my foreign friends – that Diwali puja is traditionally done in the evening, and we keep awake till midnight anyway, waiting for Lakshmiji. The belief is that at twelve o'clock midnight, when it is pitch-dark everywhere on a new moon day, She visits Her devotees and showers Her blessings on those households where there is the glitter and glamour of lights and the clatter of coins symbolising Her presence. That is why in many households flash is played with money as a ritual.

With the prospect of the children coming home, we started the preparations to welcome the Mother Goddess, Lakshmiji, and our children with great enthusiasm. I prepared all the traditional sweets and savouries, and all the food that the children liked. Early on that Friday morning my husband and I cleaned the house, made the children's beds and started decorating the house ready for puja. We arranged lights all over the house, made the rangoli and all the preparations necessary for puja. At about 1.30 p.m. our son, Dnyanesh, phoned from Oxford and told us that he and his wife were just starting from their home and should reach Manchester in about two and a half hours' time. They hoped to reach at Aberystwyth by about 8 or 9 p.m. We were overjoyed.

We finished all the housework, cooking, cleaning, decorating, and everything else that needed to be done for their arrival, by 8 p.m. and waited to receive our Lakshmi *bahu*, Seema, and our dear sons and daughter Shri Nidhi. It went passed 8, 8.30, 9, 9.30, 10, 10.30 . . . We started getting a bit worried and speculating why were they so late. Maybe they had to spend extra time at a service station, maybe they had been held up in a traffic jam, or perhaps they had been delayed in starting from Manchester itself. But if they were late in starting from Manchester, they would have phoned. We tried not to worry too much, but then it went past 11 and then 1130. There was no sign of the children – no telephone call, no message, nothing – nothing at all. We started worrying seriously now. The children would normally have phoned every two hours or so – whenever they stopped for a cup of coffee or anything else – but we had heard nothing from them since 5.30, when they were starting from Manchester after picking up my younger son, Rajul. We were sure that they would reach home at the expected time, but after 11.30 p.m., when we did not hear anything from them, all types of misgivings started rising in our minds. Had their car broken down? Had they had an accident? Had they had an unexpected mishap?

All types of worries started crowding into our heads.

My husband and I both stood at the window overlooking the road and the entrance to our driveway and fervently started praying to God for the safety of our children. What else could we do? Should we take a taxi and go out in search of them? Our car was with our children. It was bitterly cold and pitch dark outside on that 30th of November, the near new-moon night of Diwali. In the Welsh hills the strong sea wind goes piercing right into the bones especially at night. We felt like taking a taxi and going out in search of our children, but we were not sure if a taxi would oblige at that late hour without our previously arranging for it. By the way, in those days there was only one taxi service in Aberystwyth – that of Mr Roberts. Nowadays there are several more. Mr Roberts was an elderly person and we did not have the guts to wake him up in the middle of the night just like that. We felt utterly helpless. Should we start phoning the police and the hospitals? What should we do? We were at our wits' end! Prayers were our only hope, but I was finding it difficult to concentrate on God or on prayers. But what else was there to do? We seemed to have nothing in our power except to pray to the Lord and ask for His help. So that is exactly what we did. We both started praying fervently, standing in our window, with our eyes fixed on the road, and ears listening for the telephone in case the children or police or hospital rang us.

Misgivings of all sorts arose in our minds. Had they had a serious accident and were in no position to call us? Or perhaps something else had happened. My elder son had only a second-hand car – maybe it had broken down, or perhaps the wayside telephones were not working! Our misgivings were running wild, anticipating any kind of emergency.

I don't think I had ever before prayed so earnestly or so fervently in all my life. Please, God! Please save our children! Please, God! Help them if they are in trouble. Please, God! Save them from any mishap. My husband stood silent at the window, his heart attuned to God. I said all the prayers I knew for the safety and protection of our children. The situation and the wait were becoming unbearable. Each passing moment seemed like a year gone by. The suspense was choking. It was getting colder and darker by the minute. The ice-cold winter winds howling at our windows and doors seemed to be tearing apart our hearts more than the trees and branches outside the house. Our anxiety for our children had assumed a frightening magnitude. Every minute passed like an hour. It was past twelve o'clock midnight – no sign of the children yet. It went past 1 a.m. after midnight – still no sign of them, no phone call or any message from anyone! God! What were we to do? With worry in our hearts, eyes on the road and ears on the phone we prayed to God, as deeply as we could, to please help our children wherever they were in whatever predicament.

Then, at about 1.40 a.m. or so, in the middle of the dark night, at last we saw a ray of light and a ray of hope. A car was coming along our road. It looked like our son's car, and lo and behold! it was indeed his car, with our children in it. Thank God! We breathed a sigh of relief and rushed down to open the door for them.

We thanked God with all our hearts.

The children were very cold and very hungry and very tired. So we served the dinner straight away. No Diwali puja could we do that night. During the dinner we asked our children why they had been so much delayed and why they had not phoned us. (There were no mobile phones in those days.)

This is what they told us: When they were nearing Shrewsbury they realised that they were running out of petrol. They thought they would fill up at Shrewsbury where there is a big petrol station, but unfortunately by the time they reached there the petrol station had closed. In Wales in those days, in the winter season, everything used to shut down by 6 o'clock in the evening – even petrol stations. They looked for a self-service one, but had no luck. They kept on driving, hoping that the car might just oblige and carry them home or somewhere near, from where they could just walk the rest of the way. Unfortunately that was not to be. Just about thirty-five miles away from our home, near Rhayader, the car simply stopped. It refused to go further. The tank was totally empty.

They looked for a telephone booth to inform us, but on that stretch of road they could find none. They knew that the nearest petrol pump was at least twenty miles away. The tank was totally empty. It would not drag them another yard. They looked for a bed-and-breakfast place or any house which would allow them to make a phone call home. In those days in those Welsh mountains the area was only thinly populated. They ran up and down, in the hills and valleys, wherever they saw a flicker of light, but on that cold, wintry, dark night nobody would open their door for them – not even where there was a bed-and-breakfast sign.

Depressed, disappointed and disheartened they returned to the car and resigned themselves to their fate of spending the night on the open road under the dark and cold sky and shimmering stars, inside their car. They had no petrol so there was no heating inside the car. It was about 11 p.m. by then. They tried to wrap themselves up in their overcoats as best as they could, but the cold was unbearable and overwhelming. What could they do to save themselves from the freezing cold? Soon they had an ingenious idea. Three of them would push the car and one would steer it. The exercise and toil would not only keep their bodies warm and save them from freezing inside the car but also get them nearer home. So that is exactly what they did. Three of them pushed the car in turns and one steered it. That is how they managed as best as they could to keep themselves warm enough to stop being frozen inside the car on the open road.

Soon they figured out that if they pushed the car uphill, it would automatically roll down the hill without having to start the engine or pushing from outside all the time. That way they not only kept themselves warm but also covered a distance of about twenty miles. At last they managed to reach our family's favourite garage at Ponterwyd, which had a self-service pump and which was only about ten miles away from our home. It was about 1.15 a.m. by then.

Quickly my older son took out the one-pound note that he had in his pocket. The note had become quite crumpled up in his overcoat pocket. (In those days there were no pound coins, only notes.) He straightened it out in his hands and inserted it into the slot of the self-service pump. They got enough petrol to drive them up to Aberystwyth and home.

We were extremely grateful to God and also to the lady who ran the garage with a self-service facility. Because of them, our children could reach home instead of languishing on the open road shivering in the cold, hungry and thirsty.

Next day, after breakfast I said to my husband, "Let us go and fill up the tank in our children's car so that they don't have to face the same ordeal as they had to face on their way home. Back in the seventies in Wales the garages remained closed on Sundays in the winter, so it was essential to go on the Saturday itself. To me it was a matter of the utmost urgency.

We decided to go to the same garage where they had filled up the night before. I not only wanted to go there to thank the lady, but also because, as I have already said, that was our family's favourite garage. It sold a lot of typical Welsh goods, like Welsh tweed purses, skirts, mufflers, blankets and many other craft and art things, including objects made of local slate from the nearby quarry and gifts made of local wood, brass and glass. Our daughter-in-law loved going there, so she and our sons came along with us.

While my husband and my older son were filling up the petrol I thought I would go and thank the lady, the owner of the garage (with whom I was already quite friendly), for keeping a self-service pump.

I had hardly finished saying my sincere thanks when the lady looked at me from top to bottom in astonishment and asked, "What are you talking about? That pump has been out of order for a long time. It has been rusting away for the past six months. Moreover, there is no petrol below that pump."

I said, "I do not know about that, but my children got the petrol all right last night."

She was amazed. She looked at me again in sheer astonishment, not quite believing what I was telling her. She called her partner out of the shop and asked me to tell him what I had just told her. They just shook their heads again and again, apparently not believing what I was trying to tell them, so I called my son to verify that what I was telling them was true. He told them the same thing as I had told them, but still they would not believe us.

At last the lady told my son, "Show me what you did and how you got the petrol?"

My son took out a nice new one-pound note and inserted it into the slot of the self-service pump. As she expected, no petrol came out.

She said triumphantly, "See, I told you. This pump does not work; there is no petrol below it."

Now it was our turn to be astonished. We all looked at the pump and at her, quite bewildered. My son tried again, but still no petrol came out. Then he crumpled up the note to make it like the one he had used the night before. Still the pump did not oblige. It stood as dry as a stump, just as the owners expected. He tried again with an old crumpled-up note but not a drop of petrol came out. The lady felt triumphant, but we were dumbfounded. How had the pump yielded petrol on the previous night? How had the petrol come out from the very same old rusted pump? How had my children got enough petrol from an old broken-up machine? Now the lady and everyone else looked at one another in sheer bewilderment. Nobody could explain or understand how it could have happened But it had happened. My children had got just about enough petrol to bring them home safely and to save them from freezing on that cold, dark, wintry, windy night.

We had vaguely heard stories – more in mythology than in real life – of how God takes different guises to help His devotees. Had God Himself come in some disguise and poured the petrol out of that dried-up pump, to help our children out of that ordeal? How was it that an old rusted pump yielded just enough petrol for our children to reach home? How did it happen? Who made it happen? Who made the impossible possible?

Was it the power of our prayers or was it a miracle?

I think it was the power of prayer that brought about that miracle. It was a true miracle to everybody then, and it seems even more so now when I think of it. I think our prayers were heard; I have come to believe firmly that sincere prayers from the heart can work miracles. We thanked the Lord with all our hearts and celebrated Diwali as we had never celebrated before. We had a blissful feeling that the Mother Goddess, Lakshmiji, had truly blessed our family that Diwali night and made it a memorable one by lighting the divine lamp of hope and prayer in our hearts and home.

THE ADVENTURES OF MY VERY FIRST TRIP TO AMERICA

My very first trip to America was way back in 1959. In those days not many Indians went to foreign lands. It was only after the Second World War, when the Europeans and the Americans realised that they had lost a lot of their manpower, that they opened up their gates to people from Third World countries to come and help them revive their economies and industries. They wanted lots of scholars, scientists, teachers, professors and workmen to get their countries going again. Lots of scholarships were announced and lots of exchange programmes were arranged.

My husband, who was working as a professor in the Gokhale Institute of Pune at that time was asked time and again to go as an exchange professor to Harvard University, Cambridge, USA. It was an offer that many would have jumped at; but, due to his family responsibilities, my husband had been turning down the offer continuously for the past two or three years.

In 1957 my father-in-law came to stay with us in Pune. He took my husband to task, saying that people were trying so hard to go to America but he was refusing to go? Why? "One should never miss an opportunity when it knocks," he said. "Go, and tell the institute that you will accept the offer. Do not worry about your family. I am here and I shall look after them."

My husband did not have the guts to disobey his father's orders and advice, so at long last he consented and gave the institute the go-ahead to start the paperwork for his assignment as an exchange professor at Harvard University.

Everything was arranged by June 1959, and he was due to proceed to America by the first week of September, when the term started there. However, as luck would have it, on the eve of the 17th of July my father-in-law was suddenly taken ill. He had a massive stroke and passed away quietly on the morning of the 19th of July. It was like a bolt from the blue for us. We were shocked and stunned beyond measure. It was so sudden and so unexpected! My husband went into a state of utter depression and confusion.

When ultimately he got over the initial shock, the America question again hung heavy in front of him. What was he to do now? Should he or should he not go to America? If he went, what would happen to his young family? Where would we stay? If he did not go, it would be disrespecting his father's last wishes and letting down the institute as well. After much thought and contemplation, and consultation with the institute's seniors, he realised that it would not be easy to refuse the offer now that everything had been finalised.

I too gave him the reassurance that we should be all right here in India. I would gladly have gone to my father's house, but my elder sister with all her kids was already staying there as her husband was sent to the UK on government assignment for two years. I did not want to be an added burden on my father's household, so I decided to rent a house in Delhi and live somewhere near to our other relatives.

I really did not want to go to a foreign land with three small kids, where I knew that I would have to do all the dirty boring household chores by myself without any help of any kind. So, reluctantly, my husband started his preparations for the long journey and finally proceeded to America alone in the first week of September as arranged. We had both agreed that, after all, two years is not such a long time and we would somehow manage.

My husband had been away only five or six months when one fine March morning I received a telegram from him: 'Stay extended. Arrange your and children's passport. Letter follows.' The letter did come but it gave no specific reason why the stay was extended or why he wanted us to come, only an urgent request to join him as early as possible. We were somewhat worried. I thought maybe he was not keeping well, or not eating well, or simply missing his family. Whatever the reason may have been, we had to get around to getting our passports prepared as early as possible, and we started with the rest of the preparations in right earnest.

In those days not many people used to go to America from India. Far fewer ladies than men went, and even fewer ladies with children. I was the first lady in the whole of our extended families to go to America – the dreamland of many Indians. No one else had been there except my own older brother who had been to America in 1947 but he was living far away in Bombay, in those days. Only he could have given me some advice based on experience. However, suggestions of all sorts started pouring in from everybody around. Only one of them seemed somewhat sensible, and that was to take enough shoes for my children to last for two years – the tentative period of our stay there. "Shoes" they said, "are very expensive in America."

So off I went to my grandparents' house in Agra, where in those days Baluja shoes were renowned for their workmanship, design and durability. I bought for each child two pairs of their size at that time and three, four sizes ahead, like if their size was three then I also bought sizes four, five and six respectively for each child. I bought several pairs of shoes and sandals for myself as well, in various colours and the latest designs, with the result that I had about thirty to thirty-five pairs of shoes alone – enough to fill up a large suitcase. I also bought a lot of Indian groceries to take with me, like lentils of all kinds, black grams, gram flour, semolina, *poppadoms* and a whole load of other Indian spices and condiments – more than a whole boxful. I did all this shopping because my husband had written not to bring more than two or three sets of clothes for the children because we could buy children's clothing in America itself. So all that I had to carry was my own clothes, which fitted nicely into one suitcase only. In the children's baggage allowance of twenty kilograms each, I decided to take all those things mentioned above.

Now the big task of packing everything for the air journey began. After having spent extravagantly on all those things, I realised that I did not have enough cash left to buy leather suitcases. Metal trunks were out of question as they are very heavy and not suitable for air travel. My brother-in-law, i.e. my *jijaji*, suggested that as Kashmir wickerwork boxes are very light and sturdy they would be ideal to carry shoes and groceries, etc. –and they are available at a reasonable price. My elder sister, Radhe Jiji, and her husband, Jagbir Singh Jijaji, helped me to do the shopping and the packing. After fitting up everything properly into the boxes, Jijaji realised that they were too heavy and might break on the journey, so he went and bought some big bundles of strong thin rope and tied them around the wickerwork boxes. He used several rounds of the rope lengthwise and several rounds breadthwise and at each joint he tied a strong knot. Jijaji was a perfectionist: whatever he did, he did with perfection. So our suitcases were nicely packed and tightly secured. Our tickets, sent from America by my husband, had also arrived.

The big day came sooner than we had realised. We drove to the airport with several of our relatives, who all wanted to say goodbye and see us take off. As we approached the airport building I noticed several vendors selling ripe, juicy, mouth-watering mangoes right outside the gate of the airport. I wished I could take some for my husband, who loved mangoes, but my baggage allowance was already full, according to the scales of the coal depot at the back of our house. We had to send our boxes and suitcases there wrapped up in old sheets, to save them from getting black from the coal which lay all over the place for weighing. In those days we did not have a weighing scale at our home, and I did not know of anybody else who had one in their home, so every time we put in something or took out something, or rearranged our boxes by putting in titbits here and there, they had to be sent to our local coal depot at the back of our house to be weighed. The crude scales of the depot had showed that our baggage allowance of eighty kilograms for all four of us was complete. So, however tempting the mangoes looked, I had to suppress the desire to buy some for my husband.

Once inside the airport we had to rush to the check-in desk. To my great surprise and delight I saw that my luggage was a good six or seven kilograms short of the allowance. Immediately the thought rushed through my mind, 'Why not take mangoes in that remaining allowance?' I turned to my younger brother, Omesh, who had been helping me all through my preparations and had come with us to the airport, I asked him to run fast, buy a shoulder bag from the airport shop and fill it up with best-quality mangoes. With great efficiency he accomplished the task before it was time for us to go to the security check. I had not the slightest idea that things like mangoes would not be allowed into the USA. If I had, I would not have even thought of buying them.

With mixed feelings and watery eyes we bade farewell to all the relatives who had come to see us off at the airport and followed the flow of the passengers proceeding to the security check.

Once inside the departure lounge, a strange feeling of being alone with just my children in the waiting area overtook me, in spite of being surrounded by people all around. But they were all total strangers. I wished I had my husband with me! He could have at least looked after the children, who now got interested in exploring the area. They ran to the big glass windows, from where they could see the planes standing by their gates or landing or taking off from the runway. It was all very amusing to them, but I was finding it hard to keep an eye on our hand baggage as well as all the three of them at the same time.

Anyway, boarding was announced and we boarded the plane – a Boeing 707, the latest and the biggest passenger plane at that time from Palam Airport, New Delhi.

It was past 1.30 a.m. when the plane took off. We were all excited and very well looked after by the beautiful young air hostesses, but we had a few anxious moments because of rough weather and there were several air pockets just before and after Frankfurt. We reached London safely at about 8.30 a.m. the next morning. All passengers were asked to disembark from the plane with their hand baggage, so that the plane could be cleaned for the next leg of the journey to New York. I had three small kids with me half asleep, half awake so I asked the air hostess if I could leave the children's toys and blankets, etc. on the plane as I had to carry my daughter in my lap. She said it was OK but I must take my purse and the tickets with me. With my daughter on my left shoulder, my heavy travelling handbag on my right shoulder, and the two boys (six and seven and a half years old) tugging on my sari from both sides, I was the last person to get down from the plane.

As soon as I stepped onto the ground a gentleman in a blue uniform asked me for my tickets. Innocently I handed over my tickets to him, thinking that must be the airport regulation and that everybody before me must have also done so. After handing over my tickets I rushed to the bus, which was waiting just for us, as all the other passengers were already seated, in the bus – which was to take us to a restaurant for lunch. It was all so strange: new faces, new places, new country, new customs! London – so very different from India.

The bus drove us to a hotel, which to me seemed quite far from the airport. I followed the other co-passengers as they walked through the long corridors of the hotel, making an effort to remember some of the faces and their dresses so that I could follow them back from the hotel to the bus and to the airport. I admit that I was feeling quite nervous being on my own with three little kids to look after, especially as I had never been a very outgoing person, right from my schooldays through college till after marriage. I had never travelled alone before and going to such a far-off country with the added responsibility of the kids was quite an unnerving task for me.

The long and winding corridors of the hotel leading to the dining room seemed like a maze to me. The hotel itself was big and busy. The dining room looked more like a transit lounge than a dining place. There was a host of people scurrying around, some looking for suitable tables and some rushing back to their flights. Others were sitting leisurely enjoying their meals.

Fortunately I found an empty table and sat down with my children, rather ill at ease. The thought of whether I would be able to get back to my plane was continuously worrying me. The children were uncomfortable because of the cold.

I had no idea that London would be so cold in the hot month of June. In India it is very hot in June, but still we normally have hot breakfasts and hot lunches; but in this cold country the food served was even colder – chilled pineapple juice, chilled melon slices, cold slices of bread and cold meat. I managed to have a sip of the juice but the children did not touch a thing. Anyway, the food was not important; important was that we didn't lose sight of our co-passengers. As soon as we saw the first group of people from our flight leaving their table we got up too, without eating a morsel of food, and trailed them back up to the aircraft.

We waited for our turn to board the plane, but as soon as I put my foot on the first step of the ladder the air hostess, or some other lady in uniform stopped me and wanted to see my tickets. I was taken aback.

"Why," I said, "the tickets are already with you people."

"What?" she asked in surprise.

I told her that someone had asked for my tickets when I was leaving the plane, and I had handed over our tickets to him.

She looked somewhat worried and told me off, saying, "You should never part with your tickets." Then, after a little pause, she enquired, "Was the man wearing a uniform?"

I said, "Yes, he was wearing a blue uniform."

Her next question was, "Could you recognise him?"

I was not too sure of that.

With some concern she said, "Sorry, but we can't allow you to board this plane."

It was like a bolt from the blue. "Why?" I asked in utter amazement.

"Because" she said "you do not have your tickets."

I tried to make her understand that I had the tickets with me all right until I was asked to hand them over to the person collecting them at the base of the ladder. I took it for granted that everyone else before me must have also done so. As I have already mentioned, I was the last person to disembark from the plane. I had not actually seen anybody handing over their tickets to anybody, but I had just assumed that the person who asked for my tickets must have collected them from the others as well. I pleaded hard with the lady to please let me board the plane.

The lady refused to listen to anything I was telling her. Some other airport officials joined her and almost forcefully dragged my children and me to a cold, solitary room in a nearby building as if we were criminals. The only furniture there was a bare wooden bench. She asked us to sit down on the bench, but who wanted to sit down there! I simply wanted to rush back to our plane. The three children had started crying when they had stopped us from boarding the plane. Now they started crying really loudly. Hearing their loud cries, two or three more air hostesses came and tried to soothe them, but to no avail. I was confused and worried, and with great difficulty was holding my own tears back. How could I have consoled them?

After a while, the air hostess who had stopped us boarding the plane paraded three or four people in front of us and asked me to identify the one who had taken our tickets. It was impossible for me to single out the one who had taken our tickets. To me, in that state of mind, every Englishman in a blue uniform looked the same. I could not pin point any one of them. By this time the children were really howling loudly. I told the air hostesses, with as much calm as I could muster, to take me to the plane. There I thought I might be able to recognise the one who had taken our tickets from us among those doing different odd jobs around the plane.

By this time the air hostesses had become quite sympathetic, and perhaps a bit nervous too because of the children's continuous crying. Eventually they agreed to take me near to the plane, but unfortunately even there I could not recognise the man who had robbed me of my tickets. The air hostesses felt sorry for me, but said firmly that there was no way they could allow me to board the plane without my tickets. All my pleas to let me board my plane were of no avail. I think now, as I am writing, that the boarding passes must have been still with me and seeing them they might have allowed us on the plane, but that's what happens when you are nervous, tired and confused and travelling alone for the first time by air and do not know the importance of those little slips. I now wonder why they themselves did not ask for them! Maybe if they had asked, the situation might not have got so serious, and bitter, but what had to be, had to be.

I was exhausted, tired and desperate. The children's continuous crying was compounding the confusion. I had no option but to give in to the orders of the authorities.

In the end I had to tell them, "OK, if you don't allow me to board the plane, then you will have to do two things: First you must inform my husband waiting at the New York airport that I am not coming by this flight; second you must take down all my luggage from the plane, including the hand luggage left behind on our seats, because" I said, "I cannot stay here in London without the children's clothing and also without my own clothes with me."

This set them to do some hard thinking. My requests were very reasonable. They too realised that it would be unethical to detain me in London without informing my husband and without a change of clothes. The plane had already been delayed by more than an hour or so in the hassle and taking my luggage down from the plane's belly would delay it even more. This would put all the other passengers to even greater inconvenience and frustration. It was very, very inconvenient to themselves as well to bring everybody's luggage down and sort out mine from hundreds of other suitcases.

After long consultations among themselves and much thinking, they said, "All right, you may board the plane."

I heaved a sigh of relief and the children stopped crying, though extremely tired and hungry they were.

Thus we started the second leg of our eventful journey, exhausted, frustrated, miserable and worried. 'What if they wouldn't allow us out of the airport without our tickets?' 'What would my husband think?' 'Would he be there in New York from Boston in time to meet us?' 'How would he reach there – by plane, by bus or by train?' 'What if his train is late?' All these mumble-jumble thoughts hovered in my mind. I wished I could get some sleep and rest my mind.

Ultimately our plane took off from Heathrow at about seven in the evening instead of four in the afternoon. I hoped that once they finished with the dinner it would be night and I should be able to get some sleep. But where was the night? The bright shining sun was always ahead of us. It was continuous day for us for thirty-six hours without the interval of night between the two days. What an experience! All through the journey, wherever we were, the Sun was always ahead of us! This was a very new and a very strange experience for me.

We reached New York early the next morning. I think everybody from our plane was quite tired, like me, but somehow like automatic locomotives they all started moving to the luggage carousels. I joined the flow of fellow passengers.

At about 10 a.m. I found myself face-to-face with the American customs officials. All three of them on that table looked at me rather amused – an Indian lady in a sari with three kids and an assortment of luggage the like of which they had perhaps never before seen. Who travels to America with such clumsy wickerwork boxes? I could read on their faces that they were quite puzzled and suspicious about me.

Then, sternly, one of them asked me, "What is there in those boxes?"

I told them truthfully what was in them, but apparently they did not believe me. They ordered me to open up the wickerwork boxes. As I leaned down to open one, it became apparent that they had smelt something. 'Sniff-sniff' they went.

There was so much new leather and so many different pickles and spices in the boxes that I thought it was no wonder they were getting the smell of it.

I tried as hard as I could to undo the tight knots my brother-in-law had tied to secure the mesh of ropes. As I bent down, my shoulder bag of mangoes came closer to their noses. The strong smell of the somewhat overripe mangoes by now made them even more suspicious.

They asked me rather sternly, "Is there any plant or vegetable matter in there?"

Suddenly it dawned on me that it might be the mangoes that they had smelt not shoes and spices. By the time we had reached New York the children had felt warm and had taken off their woollen jumpers, which I had casually put over the bag of mangoes because there was no room or time to put them elsewhere. At the New York Airport, I had also put my shawl over the bag without any deliberate intention of hiding the mangoes. Now I became cautious and kept the bag where it was, on my back out of their sight.

Well, anyway, I had tried as hard as I could to undo the knots, but I could not even manage to loosen the very first one. The customs officials were losing their patience with me. In exasperation they pulled the bag away from me towards them and tried to undo the knots themselves. Believe me, it was no easy task for them either. They had to work really hard to undo each knot. It was a sight to see. The strange mixed smell of leather shoes and ripe mangoes was driving them crazy. I felt sorry for them, because the knots were never intended to be undone. Jijaji had told me to simply cut the ropes off on reaching home. None of us had the slightest inkling that they might have to be opened up at customs.

Suddenly the children shouted, "Dada!"

I looked around and saw my husband standing on the balcony above, among the crowd of people who had come to meet their relatives or friends. He, along with others, was watching the whole process with great amusement and taking a movie of the whole drama. What a relief! God! My whole tension dissolved in an instant. We were relieved, but not the customs officials.

It had taken them almost an hour to open up all thirty-six knots on one case alone. It must have seemed to them like victory at last – but wait! not quite yet. They had another hurdle to cross, and that was to open up each little wrapping inside the case; and what did they find inside each little wrapping? No mangoes for sure, but shiny little shoes. (I had thrown away the shoeboxes to save space and reduce the weight). In sheer disgust they pushed the box to one side.

Then they turned their attention to the other box and asked me, "Now what is there in this one?"

I said, "Open it up." I knew they would not believe whatever I may tell them.

It was a daunting task for them, but the strong smell of ripe mangoes was not to be ignored. They had to do their duty. They resigned themselves to the tedious task of opening the tight knots of the other wickerwork box. By the time they undid the last knot they were literally perspiring and terribly disappointed because the smell of mangoes had suddenly disappeared and instead the strong smell of freshly ground Indian spices – red chilli powder, turmeric, ground cumin and coriander – poppadoms and a whole load of Indian condiments, pickles, etc. filled their nostrils. They did not know what to do and what to say. Examining around a few packets and feeling quite confused, they enquired, "Is everything in here fried?"

Somehow the inner voice inside me impelled me to say, Yes, to save them from further embarrassment and to get the whole thing over as soon as possible. The children were impatient to run to their dad and I was anxious to save the precious bag of mangoes, which fortunately they had been unable to discover so far. I did not want to embarrass them further.

To my great relief, they said, "You can go now."

But how could I go with the boxes' lids still flung wide open? Gently but firmly I requested them to please close the boxes and tie up the ropes again. They looked disgruntled, but they felt they had to do it.

At long last the ordeal was over and I was with my husband again. I could breathe the refreshing air of the new dreamworld – New York, America at last! Hurray!

Soon I realised my husband was not the only one who had come to receive us. There were at least twenty-five people with him, who had all travelled from Boston to New York just to receive us. It was hard for me to believe that my husband had become such a popular

person in such a short time – a period of just about six months.
"*Bhabiji, namaste, Bhabiji, namaste.* Welcome, Bhabiji. *Aiyea! Aiyea!*"

I had never expected such a warm welcome. Everything was so exiting and strange! I had never known this sort of welcome before and I found it difficult to take it all in. I was really happily surprised when everyone from all sides tried to introduce themselves. I was overwhelmed by such a warm welcome by so many people.

Soon I was made aware that my husband had been elected President of the Indian Association of America. That was indeed a big honour, and I certainly received a fitting welcome for the first lady of the Indian community of the USA.

It was past 2 p.m. when our cavalcade of seven or eight cars started from New York to Boston. A lavish dinner was waiting for us at home prepared by Mrs Ezekiel, the wife of one of my husband's friends and colleagues at Harvard.

A whole year passed by happily. Each passing day brought new delights, new joys new experiences. The days rolled by smoothly. Living a lively life, I never really bothered to investigate why we were summoned to America in such a hurry!

It was after quite some time that I came to know the reason. The reason was– well, try to guess. No, I'm sure you can't. Well, you know America – how free and how ambitious the people are over there, especially the younger generation! Now, no sooner had my husband started his work at the university than the young blondes started approaching him, and some even tried to become more intimate with him. After all, he was young, handsome and intelligent and a professor at such a young age. When the girls came to know that he had been elected President of the Indian Association of America the pressure grew. No amount of telling them that he was already married and even had kids would convince them. None of the beauties would believe his words. They just thought that he was making up stories to fob them off.

In the end he realised that there was no other way to escape from them than to call us in person in front of their eyes – hence the urgency in his calls. Well, whatever the reason, we had a great time. That first trip to America was extremely eventful. It changed our lives for ever – and for the better, I think.

THE WASHERMAN AND THE PANTHER

It was the year 1950. We were living in Udaipur in those days. In 1947 my father was invited by the then Maharaja of Udaipur for the post of Chief Engineer for Irrigation. Udaipur is famous for its natural beauty and its numerous lakes. Our bungalow was situated in between two beautiful lakes on a hill. In front of it was the beautiful blue Fateh Sagar Lake and at the back was the oblong green Swaroop Sagar Lake. I should not write 'was' because the lakes and our bungalow are still there, only we do not live there any more.

The Maharaja's official guest house, 'the Laxmi Vilas Palace', was opposite to our bungalow across the road on another hill. My maternal uncle, Mr R. B. L. Mathur, who had recently retired as the Accountant General of India from the Central Government Service, was also invited by the Maharaja in 1949 to look after the financial affairs of his state. As the job was for a limited period only, Mamaji had not brought his family and was staying as a guest of the Maharaja in the Laxmi Vilas Palace.

Mamaji used to start his day with a morning walk by the Fateh Sagar Lake, which had beautiful white railings all along its shore on the main road. The white-painted waist-high railing doubled the beauty of the lake as well as the road. The road was quite broad, though there was not much traffic in those days, especially during the early hours of the morning. On the other side of the road next to the Laxmi Vilas Palace was the vast unexplored, thickly forested jungle, full of wildlife of all sorts, including panthers which were in largest number there in those days.

One day, very early in the morning, we heard a desperate loud knock at our front door, which opened into the sitting room. My father and I both got up with a start and, realising the urgency of the knock, I ran towards the door. My father got there first, his bedroom being adjacent to the sitting room. Hurriedly he undid the latch and opened the door. To our great surprise we saw our Mamaji standing at the door shivering from head to foot

"*Arre Bhai Sahib. Aap!*"

"So early in the morning? Why? What is the matter?" inquired my father in astonishment, at the same time requesting him to come in and sit down.

Mamaji rushed into the sitting room and asked my father to quickly shut the door tight behind him. "Make sure it is shut tight," he begged again.

This was very unusual – not like Mamaji at all. In spite of our asking him to please sit down, he did not sit. Instead, holding on to my father's arm, Mamaji almost dragged him towards the inner rooms, motioning me as well to come inside. We were very much surprised to see Mamaji, usually a very composed and calm person, in that unusual disturbed state of mind and behaving so unnaturally. He was not only shivering and sweating but also breathless and terrified. With an urgency in his tone he requested us to take him to the back rooms.

To see Mamaji in that condition was very worrying. We had always seen him as a cheerful person and he was normally very calm and sober.

Once he sat down in the back dining room, we asked him, "What is the matter? Why are you so pale and frightened? Has anything happened in the guest house?"

Mamaji looked around towards all the doors and windows and asked us again and again if all the doors and windows were tightly shut. We assured him that yes, they were all tightly bolted up. After taking a deep breath he gathered up enough courage to speak up.

"You know, Brij Govind [my father's name], a panther is coming right behind me! It might be just outside your bungalow even now. Could you please peep out from the glass window?

Don't open it – just look from inside through the glass. It might still be there, though I sincerely pray to God that it isn't. Can you see it at all? Is he still there? I hope it is not following me any more!"

"Panther?" I asked in astonishment. "Yes! A big panther." he replied

After making sure that there was no panther around, Mamaji took a deep breath and relaxed a bit. Now we knew the reason for him being so terrified.

We could not easily believe what he was saying, but there he was, sitting in front of us, perspiring and trembling with fear.

"Was a panther really following you Mamaji?"

"Yes!" he replied frightfully.

My father tried to calm him down, saying that panthers don't normally come within the boundary wall of our bungalow.

Mamaji felt a bit relaxed and continued: "You know, I saw a very big panther swishing a dhobi [a washerman] away from right in front of my eyes. I am sure the pantheress was behind the panther ready to leap at me."

"What!" My father and I both exclaimed in astonishment.

"A pantheress trying to get at you? Where? When?" I asked in sheer disbelief.

"Just now," he said, "when I was going on my usual morning walk, I saw a dhobi walking right in front of me with a big bundle of dirty clothes on his head. He was hardly ten feet ahead of me and was walking with perfect ease, fearless of anything or

anybody. Maybe that was his daily route to the lake, where he was taking the clothes to be washed. I have never before noticed him going that way, but maybe he usually goes a bit later or earlier than me. I assume he takes the clothes routinely to wash at the end of the lake where the water flows out as a river. Today, however, I was watching him. I was glad that there was somebody else on the road besides me, because I was a bit early today. The dhobi was walking just a few feet in front of me and I was watching him with interest, thinking how well he was balancing the heavy load on his head."

"Then suddenly I saw a big panther darting out like lightning from the forest on the hill, knocked aside the dhobi's load of clothes with a slash of his front paw, grabbed the dhobi in his mouth by the neck and dragged him like a bundle back into the thick forest.

"I felt sure the pantheress was right behind the panther ready to pounce on me. She would have surely grabbed me but just then a car with its headlights on came in between the panther and me and I took the opportunity to run as fast as I could.

"The palace gate is too far to run so I dashed towards your house. I was sure your watchman would be there to help me but I did not see him, so I threw open the gate myself. I did not have the courage to stop even for a moment to shut the gate behind me. I was just too scared that it might be still following me." He pleaded again: "Please make sure again that all the doors and windows are tightly shut."

We heard Mamaji's story in breathless silence. It was a terrifying tale. Poor Mamaji – a retired, frail gentleman! No wonder he was in such a shaky state! It would frighten anybody to see a panther grabbing a man right in front of his eyes from such a close distance.

Could a pantheress be really behind him? Was he still dreaming? We had been living in that bungalow for quite a while now but had never heard such a story before. However there was no question of not believing him either.

By this time the servants were awake, and had brought hot tea for all of us. Handing over a cup of tea to Mamaji, my father started saying calmly and convincingly, "You know, Bhai Sahib, these panthers, they are definitely very canny, unpredictable wild beasts but they have a great family sense. If the panther made a kill he would share it with all his family. The pantheress would not even think of killing another victim until they finished off the first one. Your fear is baseless, so now relax and enjoy the tea."

Mamaji replied, "Yah, but that is true for lions only. Panthers are different. They are the most ferocious and cunning of all wild animals. They will attack even if there is already enough to feast upon. Don't be so sure about them."

Maybe what Mamaji said was true. Panthers may kill just for fun or fear. We had definitely heard a lot of stories about them. The hill across the road was well known for its large population of panthers, and a variety of other dangerous beasts inhabiting the thick forests on the hill, but we had never before heard of anybody actually being attacked. But there could always be a one-off case like the one Mamaji had witnessed.

My father sent out servants to make sure that no dangerous wildlife of any kind had come within the boundary walls of our bungalow. Mamaji could not pluck up courage to go back to the palace till it was broad daylight and even then he had to be escorted by our car– he still did not have the courage to cross the road on his own.

I think that after this incident Mamaji stopped going on his morning walks so early; and maybe he also stopped going by his favourite route by the lake, but started going in the opposite direction on the road leading towards the city. We never encountered any panthers in the compound of our bungalow, either before or after the incident, but a few years later the servants and the watchman reported that a hyena had given birth to her cubs in the unkempt wooded area of our compound, near the boundary wall.

POSTSCRIPT

I had such happy and unforgettable memories of Udaipur that I very much wanted my children to see the untamed, unspoiled natural beauty of the place. I persuaded my youngest daughter, Shri Nidhi, her husband, Guy Footring, and her children, dear Varun and Vikram, to come with me to Udaipur when they were visiting India during their Easter break in March 2002, but to my great disappointment things had changed drastically in the intervening fifty-eight years.

The whole hill, which used to abound with panthers, has been totally cleared of all panthers and other dangerous animals. Buildings have cropped up everywhere, including a Shivaji memorial park, a temple, a school and God knows what else!

In the centre of the beautiful Fateh Sagar Lake they have built an observatory, which has ruined the natural beauty of the lake. The lake itself has shrunk drastically because of continuous drought for the past twelve years. It is now not even one third of its former size as I had remembered it some fifty-eight years ago. Even the Singhal family's Lake View bungalow and also our own bungalow do not look quite the same.

The water level of Lake Pichola has also gone down drastically.

The Lake Palaces, which were the royal family's resorts of recreation, have been turned into hotels, but at least in this way they have been able to retain part of their royal glamour and glory.

Everything in this world is prone to change; nothing remains the same for ever. Udaipur is no exception. Everything has changed drastically, almost beyond recognition, to my great disappointment.

THE DEADLY SNAKES IN OUR GARDEN

This is an incident of the bygone years of the late forties, when I was about nineteen years old and my father had moved to Udaipur after his retirement from Central Government Service in Delhi.

In Udaipur we were allotted a big bungalow. A beautiful garden in front led down into a rugged valley below, and at the back the courtyard rose up to a high hill, all within the boundary wall of the bungalow. Not long after our occupation, we realised that the bungalow was inhabited not only by our family but by a number of other families as well, most of which were already residing there much before us. One, of course, was the family of the caretaker janitor (Jamadar) whose main work was to clean the toilets and sweep the outer mud compound all around the bungalow. Officers may have come and gone but his family lived there permanently, in one of the outhouses of the bungalow. Apart from our family and the janitor's family there were a number of other families also residing there permanently. They were the families of a variety of snakes, scorpions, toads, spiders, centipedes, lizards and very many varieties of other insects also. One time when we were there, a pair of hyenas also made part of our compound their home and their cubs were born in the thickly overgrown valley to one side of the bungalow. Once the servants reported that a crocodile was basking in the safety of our path to the bungalow instead of on the dry road outside. In addition to all these, there were many species of small and large insects, like big red ants which drew blood when they bit, grasshoppers, butterflies, moths, etc. There were also a number of beautiful birds nesting there, ranging from the tiny tailor birds to the enormous peacocks.

The predominant creatures there were the snakes and giant spiders, the like of which I have never again seen in all my life anywhere else. The smallest of those spiders were about three inches long and two and a half inches wide; the bigger ones were about four to five inches long. They were quite scary, but at the same time quite attractive to look at. I used to admire their grace and their beauty. They were shiny golden-brown in colour with hard, sharp and smooth legs which formed triangular shapes as they moved about. There were lots of them all around our bungalow in the mud compound. They were frightening but harmless. We never heard that anybody had been bitten or hurt by them.

The most dangerous creatures were the deadly snakes of all sizes, ranging from the tiny ones to the giant fifteen or sixteen feet-long ones. Most of them were cobras but there were very many other species as well, in different colours from gold to silvery-black to brown to dark blackish-maroon to yellow with shell-patterned backs. All the different species had different patterns on their backs.

'The land belongs to snakes' is a common saying in India. They are found all over India, but their sightings in big cities like Delhi or Bombay are comparatively rare. To us it was simply unimaginable that snakes could be living permanently in households along with humans. Many bungalows in Delhi in our time had large gardens but there were hardly any snakes anywhere. To see a snake we had to find a snake charmer.

Snake charmers used to roam the streets of Delhi with their baskets of snakes, in the same way as some vendors have baskets of fruits and vegetables. The snakes in their baskets were no danger to the public because their poisonous fangs were already extracted out. The snake charmers would tickle a cobra and it would spread its hood and dance – that is, move its head to the tune of the snake charmer's 'been' which is a special instrument, something like a double-barrelled flute with a small gourd in the centre. That was our only acquaintance with snakes as long as we lived in Delhi.

On reaching Udaipur we were simply stunned by its natural beauty. Udaipur is situated among the Aravali Mountains, so it has a totally different landscape from Delhi. It abounds in natural beauty, with its numerous lakes and forests. The bungalow allotted to our father was on a hill with gorgeous views of the Fateh Sagar Lake in front and the Swaroop Sagar Lake at the back. A canal which ran along the right-side boundary wall of our bungalow joined the two lakes together. What was very intriguing to me at that time was that, though the two lakes were connected by the canal and so close to each other, yet the water of the two lakes was of completely different hues. Standing on the roof of our bungalow, we could clearly see both the lakes at the same time. The water of the Fateh Sagar Lake looked sky-blue while the water of the Swaroop Sagar Lake seemed to be dark-green! A wonder of nature, I used to think.

We simply loved the natural beauty around our bungalow. Having a hill at the back and a valley in the front within the boundary wall of the bungalow was very exiting, especially because the valley was covered with wild shrubs of sweet and sour small red berries called *Jhar beri*. My younger sisters used to love roaming about in the valley eating the delicious berries. There was also a badminton court on the right of the front garden. We children played badminton in the mornings as well as in the evenings and would sit there at the edge of the hill till late at night just gossiping or practising our songs with a friend of mine from the opposite bungalow who had the same music teacher as me. Anyway, what I want to say is that, though we sat there till late in the evenings, we never felt any fear of snakes or of any other creatures mentioned earlier.

In the beginning we were blissfully unaware of the existence of snakes in our garden. We – that is, my younger sisters, brother and I – even made a little 'grove' of our own by putting small pieces of rocks in a circle under a huge tree on the left side of the bungalow on the slope leading to the rocky valley below. Small shrubs don't grow under big trees, so the land was comparatively clear; even so my sisters used to sweep the enclosed area themselves, brushing aside the fallen leaves or feathers of the different birds that used to gather under the tree to eat its fruit. We used to spread a rug on the mud floor and kept a *gow takiya* or *masnad*, which is a big, round, oblong pillow, for comfort. My sisters used to call it their summer house. I used to love sitting there, not only for my studies but also to admire those sweet little birds and the majestic peacocks with their beautiful long colourful tails, which they occasionally opened up in a semicircle. Seeing all those birds eating and hearing them chirping melodiously was a feast to the eyes and ears. We were told by the permanent servants who lived there that the fruit – something like a hazelnut – was poisonous to humans but a delicacy to the birds, especially to the peacocks.

It was during this time sitting in my 'grove' that I had my first inkling that there were snakes in the vast compound. Occasionally I could hear the hissing of snakes from the nearby bushes, and once I heard a whistling sound, 'Shoooon', coming from under the bushes by the hedge. I was sure that the whistling sound was of a snake because I remembered hearing from my mother that snakes whistle. After that I became alert and kept my eyes and ears open in case I heard the whistling or hissing of a snake again, but in the first few months of summer I never heard or saw any snake at all, big or small.

It was only when the rainy season started that the servants started reporting snake sightings – first only occasionally, then quite frequently. As the days passed by, the snake sightings became much more frequent in the daytime, and their sounds at night. During the monsoon season when there are frequent showers at night we had to stop sleeping in the open courtyard at the back and had to sleep in the side veranda, the outside wall of which was thickly covered by a dense ivy. We started hearing strange sounds coming from the ivy, like 'chut, chut, chut turrrr' or just the 'chut, chut, chut' without the 'turrrr', in addition to the whistles of the snakes from different corners of the compound. We wondered what those sounds could be? On enquiring we were told that all those sounds were of different species of snakes. That was really frightening, but there was no way we could get rid of all the snakes of all the different species that lived in that bungalow.

The servants invariably used to kill any snake that they saw.

Actually the sweeper man was quite an expert in the art of killing snakes. He kept a sort of metallic hand-sized rake with sharp claws, which he would throw at a snake whenever he saw one. The rake would pin it down to the ground so that it could not run away, while he and other servants brought their long bamboo sticks to smash the head of the snake. There were rumours that the jamadar and his family used to eat the flesh of the snakes. I am not sure if this was true because I myself never asked the sweeper man and he himself never told anything about it.

However once I was greatly disappointed when the servants shrank back instead of coming forward to kill a certain comparatively small snake.

As I have already mentioned in some of my earlier articles, that I had lost my mother when I was only about eleven or twelve years old. My older sisters and brother were married and living outside of Udaipur. I was the oldest unmarried child at that time and was sort of in charge of running my father's household.

In those days, food used to be cooked on firewood stoves. Sometimes the wood gave off a lot of smoke – especially in the rainy season, when the sticks tended to get damp. So to avoid the smoke polluting the bungalows, the English gentry built their kitchens at a distance from the main building. Our bungalow was built by an English doctor known as Mr Robertson. On his retirement, he went back to Britain and the Maharaja of Udaipur bought his bungalow to use as accommodation for government officials. However, it was still known as Robertson's Bungalow. Our father had been allotted this bungalow when the Maharaja had invited him to Udaipur. The kitchen was about twenty feet away from the back veranda of the main building.

In between the veranda and the kitchen, just to the left of the kitchen door was a big 'flame of the forest' tree, which in season used to get completely covered with bunches of tiny bright beautiful red flowers with scanty, dainty, dark-green leaves peeping in-between. To this big tree our cook used to tie the family cow for milking in the evening. Around the cow and the calf there used to be a lot of fodder of long, dried, yellow strands of grass.

It was my daily routine to go to the kitchen at about 8 p.m. each evening just to check that everything for dinner at night was prepared as asked. In those days leather shoes or slippers were not allowed inside the kitchens, because leather was considered to be impure – not to be anywhere near the foodstuff, which was prepared on the kitchen floor on mud and brick hearths. The only footwear allowed in the kitchens was *chatties* or *khadauns*. *Chatties* are open-heeled wooden slippers with thick strips of woven cotton lace (*niwad*) on the top and four buttons of rubber at the bottom – two in front and two at the back as heel and sole – leaving about a half-inch gap between the *chatti* and the floor.

Now one night when I was going for my routine inspection to the kitchen I felt a long strip of yellow grass moving away from under my *chatti*. Quickly I retreated, wondering what sort of a grass was this that it could move. It did not take me long to realise that it was no grass at all but a thin, golden-yellow spotted snake, about three or four feet long.

As soon as the realisation dawned on me, I shouted in panic, "Snake, snake!"

The kitchen servants came running out with burning sticks in their hands to kill it. The watchman and the sweeper man were also nearby, and they too rushed in fast. But lo and behold! as soon as their eyes fell on the snake they seemed to turn into statues. What happened? Why weren't they coming forward to kill it off? As soon as they spotted the snake they shrank back and stood as if frozen. Not one of them moved. Silently they just watched the snake slithering away towards the high hill behind the big tree.

Infuriated, I shouted at them, "Hey! What's this? Why don't you come forward and kill it?"

In spite of my shouting and imploring them to kill the snake, none of them moved. They stood still where they were.

In panicky hushed tone one of them managed to mutter, "Bai Sahib, please go back. Please go back."

I could not understand their strange behaviour at all. I wondered why they were behaving so strangely.

In sheer disgust I turned back, calling my father aloud: "Dadaji, Dadaji."

My father was sitting on the other side of the bungalow on the front lawn. My shouts did not reach him, but my youngest sister, who was in our bedroom (the nearest room to the kitchen) heard my shouts.

She came running out, asking, "Jiji, what is it? Wh–" Before finishing the sentence, she hurriedly turned back, slamming the door tightly behind her and shouting as if in great panic, "Dadaji, Dadaji!"

Now, this was very intriguing indeed to me. Very strange! What happened? Why did she slam the door? Why did she rush back instead of coming to me? What had frightened her so much that she had to run back in panic? For a minute it flashed through my mind that perhaps the snake I thought was climbing the hill was not going up but coming back towards her. I remember that I had felt that something was gliding away in front of the veranda.

I had heard her panic calls and so had my father. I was impatient to tell my father to come quickly and order the servants to kill the snake before it disappeared into the shrubs on the hill. My sister seemed to be in a greater urgency than me.

She rushed ahead of me, shouting, "Dadaji, Dadaji!"

Hearing her first call, my father had already left his chair. He quickly climbed the five or six steps to the bungalow, crossed the wide veranda and opened the sitting-room front door to come in. He had hardly come halfway into sitting room when my sister rushed and clung to him. I was now right behind her, anxious to know what had happened to her, and also urgently trying to report the servants for not killing the snake.

Before I could say anything my sister blurted out, almost trembling with fear, "Dadaji, there is a very big black cobra sitting coiled up with its hood high in the air as if ready to strike. It is right in front of our bedroom door in the veranda."

'Oh, God!' I thought. 'Did she see a big black cobra at the same time as I saw the thin yellow snake? Horrors!'

Still out of breath, I heard her story in utter amazement. Before my father or anybody else took any action, I was dying to relate my encounter too, but before I could start my father was already calling the servants.

It was absolutely unbelievable: two snake sightings at the same time at more or less the same place. Well, not at exactly the same place, because one was out in the open mud compound while the other was on the solid cemented floor of the veranda, but only at a distance of about ten or twelve feet apart. We knew there were snakes in the garden and in the compound, but never before had we seen a snake on the paved veranda, some eight inches above the mud floor.

Now I understood why she had slammed the door behind her and had run in panic, calling our father.

What a predicament: a small, thin, yellow, harmless-looking snake curling away from under my feet and a big king cobra sitting right in front of the bedroom door!

By now the servants had come in too. Looking at them with annoyance, I reported them to father, imploring him to tell them off for not killing the snake I had seen.

My father was aghast. "What! Did you also see a snake?" he asked in utter disbelief.

"Yes, Dadaji," I narrated my own terrifying encounter with the small snake and implored him to tell off the servants.

Angrily my father looked at them and demanded why did they not kill the serpent straight away?

The servants stood with their heads down. Eventually the cook gathered the courage to speak out: "Sir, we ask your pardon, but we could not have killed that snake."

"Why?" demanded my father.

"Sir, that was no ordinary snake. It was the king of all snakes. It was a Vasuki. We can kill any other snake but not a Vasuki."

My father was totally taken aback. "What! Do we have vasukis also in here?"

"Yes, sir. They occasionally appear, but normally they lie

hidden in the shrubs in the vast compound. We don't see them very often. Even if we see one, we do not kill it because if we kill even the tiniest vasuki, we won't be able to live in this bungalow at all – none of us."

We children had never even heard the name vasuki; my father knew the name, but perhaps had never seen one.

He asked, "How do you know that it was a vasuki?"

"Sir, the sweeper man knows about all the different snakes that dwell in our compound. He has told all of us servants about them and has strictly forbidden us from killing any of them. That is why we could not kill even the tiny one that had come in Baiji Sahiba's path. We just had to let it go. We did not dare to kill it for fear of revenge. We ask for your pardon again. We were just happy to see that Baiji Sahiba was spared. Vasukis are the deadliest of all snakes. People can be saved from any other snake bite but never from a vasuki bite. They are the rulers of all the snake kingdoms."

When the cook finished speaking, the servants started to leave but my father stopped them.

"Wait. There is a cobra around too. Be careful."

"Yes, sir. We saw it too, but it had already disappeared into the jungle before we could reach it. It is difficult to trace a black cobra in the dark. We shall take care of it when we see it in the day."

Not too long after this they killed a very big black cobra but nobody could be sure that it was the same one that my sister had seen or any other! After all, there were so many of them out there in our garden!

This is just one of the many unusual encounters we had with snakes in that bungalow. Perhaps it would take another book to recount them all.

On reflection now, after so many years, I still wonder how we or our predecessors ever managed to survive in that deadly snake-infested bungalow! Perhaps God's Grace was ever more than the number of snakes and all the other deadly creatures combined together living in that bungalow!

A SUNDAY SOON AFTER MY FATHER'S RETIREMENT

It was an unforgettable Sunday. I am not able to forget it even after so many years. Just before his retirement my father was working with the Central Government as a superintending engineer at the Public Works Department in Delhi. He still had about eight months' service left before he reached retirement age. He had accumulated exactly that many months of leave, so he took advantage of that and officially retired in February 1947.

It was about 10am on a Sunday soon after his retirement. He was taking it easy, relaxing on the easy chair in his bedroom, enjoying his bed tea with us brothers and sisters sitting around him chatting. Suddenly our cook, Hari Singh, came rushing in.

"Sahibji, Sahibji, there is a big commotion outside. The neighbours who were out on a morning walk and the servants from other households have all seen with their own eyes that a big crowd is coming towards our house. They are already on the main road; soon they might be turning into our lane."

My father was a bit startled. It was the time of partition between India and Pakistan. Any crowd was a sure sign of danger.

He looked at Hari Singh and said, "What are you waiting for here, then? Go and shut and secure the main gate immediately, and prepare for any attack."

In those days all households had some sort of defence mechanism ready in their houses. Long steel bars were attached to the frames of the main entrance doors, which could be pulled across the wooden doors to make them more difficult to break in, in case of any invasion by the rioting crowds. We also kept some small weapons for self-defence, like knives; long wooden sticks with pointed steel tips, called *bhales*; and packets of red-hot chilli powder to throw into the eyes of the invaders to stop them intruding into the rooms and killing the residents indiscriminately. These were all precautionary measures for self-defence – not for attacking anybody.

By the time the servants secured the main gate and took out the *bhales*, etc. the crowd was already in our lane and calling aloud, "Mathur Sahib, Mathur Sahib."

What was this? Who were these people? What did they want? Were they shouting to get entrance to our house? Everybody was on the alert. Soon the crowd was at our gate and knocking. We all held our breath! The knocking got louder. For a long time we did not open the door, thinking that if we do not answer their knocks, they may take it that nobody was at home and might go away somewhere else.

Just then our grandfather, who was in the bathroom, came out. When he heard the loud knocking on the gate he shouted at the servants, "Hey, where are you all? Can't you hear that somebody is knocking at the gate? Go at once. Open the gate and see who is there."

We could no longer pretend that nobody was at home.

The calls from the crowd continued "Mathur Sahib, Mathur Sahib, please open the door. We have come to see you."

My father told Hari Singh, the cook, to open the kitchen window, which opened into the lane outside, and peep out and see who they were. Bravely Hari Singh unbolted the kitchen window and peeped out through the tiny slit from behind the steel bars.

Hearing the kitchen window open, the crowd rushed towards it. Hari Singh tried to shut the window but the crowd insisted: "Please do not shut the window. Please listen to us. Give us just one minute. We want to see Mathur Sahib. Please request him to come out for a minute. We want to see him."

The servants desisted but the crowd insisted. Not being able to dissuade them Hari Singh, in whom father had the most confidence, came to my father's room and told my father, "Sahibji, they are just insisting to see you. They do not look like rioters. They have garlands and other things in their hands, which they say they have brought for you."

We were all surprised to hear this. Who could these people be?

From where had such an army of people gathered with garlands and gifts for a retired officer?

Was it a hoax to trap my father? What should we do? Should we allow the gate to be opened or should we not? After a little thought, my father asked the servant to go and ask their names.

The servant went back to the kitchen window and enquired from within what their names were.

The people in the front gave their names and pleaded with the servant: "Please tell Sahibji that we are from his office. We have come to pay our respects to him."

The servant came back and told my father accordingly.

As soon as my father heard the names, he ordered Hari Singh to go and open the gate at once, and he himself headed straight to the gate. We children followed him quietly and stood behind him in the entrance hall. What we saw and heard was unbelievable.

As soon as my father appeared at the gate, the people approached him, touched his feet and started garlanding him one by one and putting their offerings in front of him on the steps of our Daryaganj house: packets, boxes and baskets of all shapes and sizes. It looked like a scene from a temple, with my father standing on the steps like a deity on a pedestal and the worshippers coming and touching his feet and garlanding him and putting their offerings in front of him on the steps.

"What is all this?" My father asked in utter amazement.

"Sir, these are just tokens of our love and our gratitude to you. As long as you were in service, we dared not bring anything for you, because we knew that you would never accept anything from any of us. But we owe you so much. You have always helped all of us in one way or another. This is just a token of our thanks, and of our love and respect for you. We can never repay in any words or kind for all that you have always done for us. These are just small tokens of our gratitude and to convey our very best wishes to you. Now you are retired, we may never get a chance to see you again. We know that you have already left the office, but we hear that you are leaving even Delhi very soon. Please accept these tiny tokens as our farewell gifts."

"We will never have an officer like you again, sir," some of them said with tears in their eyes. "Sir, all this is nothing in comparison to what you have given to us. You are a father figure to us all. Now who is there who will listen to us? To whom shall we go with our complaints and grievances? Whom shall we approach for help? We do not know how to convey our feelings and say farewell to you."

"These are just very small tokens of our heartfelt thanks to you, with all our best wishes and blessings for your retirement. May God give you a very long life full of health and happiness! May you enjoy a very happy retired life. We have come with all our prayers for you, sir! We wish you a long life, full of health and happiness."

Such touching words, spoken with such love and sincerity! They made my father speechless. What could he say? Willy nilly he had to accept the things brought with such love and respect. All through his service time he had never accepted anything from anybody, Civil engineers were notoriously famous for accepting gifts. My father had kept himself clean of all such things. But now that he had retired it was a different thing. He could no longer favour or disfavour anybody. Nobody could hope to gain any private ends meet from a retired, outgoing officer.

Farewell parties are usually given by equals, other officials and mutual friends, but in those days farewell parties even among colleagues were not so common. The lower staff – the clerks, the stenographers, the draughtsmen, the *khallasis* (the people who keep an eye on the building material lying on a site), the *chaprasees* (the porters and the peons) and the workforce on the building sites – had neither the means nor the daring to invite an officer to his home. The whole staff in the office wanted to say farewell to my father. This was their way of saying goodbye to their departing, respected, beloved officer.

My father did not know what to do or what to say to them. How could he say no to all those people, who had gathered from all over Delhi to express their gratitude and love to their respected, retired officer who was held in high respect by one and all. He was totally overwhelmed. With tears in his own eyes, he just could not turn away the tokens of their love and blessings, so he asked the servants to take the things in, so lovingly brought by his ex-staff.

The servants got busy bringing in all the packets, baskets and boxes of sweets, etc.

Very soon the whole inner courtyard and the adjoining veranda in front of the household shrine was full of cane baskets of fruits, platters and boxes of sweets, dried fruits in beautiful presentation boxes, and bags and boxes of savouries. In the end the servants had to pile some boxes and baskets on top of the dining table.

Father asked the servants to make tea and get some savouries for all of his staff. Having brought everything in, the servants headed towards the kitchen to prepare tea; but the office staff politely refused, saying, "Sir, we do not want any tea or coffee. We have already had more than our share in what you have already done for us. We do not want anything more now. We just wanted to have a glimpse of you and pay our respects to you before you leave us."

Some of them said with tearful eyes, "Please, sir, do not forget us. We shall always be there for you if ever you need us. We just want your kind self to have a very happy retired life with your family. May God's blessings be always with you, sir! Please accept our sincere good wishes from our hearts. We may never get a chance to see you again but good wishes from our hearts will always be there with you."

So saying, they turned around and started moving off with tears rolling from their eyes. The servants were already in the kitchen making some tea, but now there was no need. Anyway there was no room left in the courtyard to call anybody in.

After seeing them all off, my father came in with his own eyes wet.

This sort of scene had never before been seen by any of our family, friends or neighbours. The crowd in front of our house had doubled. Half were the people from the office and the rest were curious neighbours, their children, their servants and any chance passers-by on the road at that time. It was the most unexpected and unimaginable scene that anybody had ever witnessed before.

Once the staff left, Father was in a very sombre mood. Not only was he feeling sad at leaving such a loving and caring staff behind, but he was overwhelmed by the trouble they had taken to come to express their gratitude. He could appreciate how much planning and thinking must have gone into organising the gathering of so many people to arrive at the same time, at the same place, on the same day, with similar gifts, without any telephones or means of communication and proper transport in those bygone days.

In the end he said aloud with watery eyes, "Everyone worships a rising sun, but who worships a sun that has already set?" He then just took a cursory glance at all the stuff the staff had brought. He was not at all interested in any of the goodies lying in front of him. What had really touched his heart were their feelings, their love and respect and their sense of gratefulness to him.

After a while he looked at my older sister and me – the oldest children of the house at that time. He asked us to open up the baskets and boxes and see what was there in them.

When we opened up all the boxes and all the baskets and all the packets, our house looked like a mini market. There were piles of bananas, apples, oranges, guavas and papayas and a variety of other fruits, loads of sweets and savouries and dried fruits. All these goodies were not only a feast to the eyes but also to the nose.

Our house was filled all at once with the delicate, delicious fragrance of Nagpur oranges, Kullu apples, mouth-watering laddus, and barfis, rasgullas and all sorts of other Bengali and North Indian sweets and savouries. The rose and marigold garlands were spreading their own sweet smell around.

Looking at all those things we realised that there was no way our family could consume them all, even in a month. What were we to do with all that stuff? There were no elderly ladies in the house to give us any advice on what to do with them. We sincerely wished our mother was there, but she had long ago been snatched by the cruel hand of destiny. The best we could think of was to call our older sister who lived in Daryaganj, not too far from our own house. So we rang her up.

Jiji and Jijaji came as soon as they could. They looked at the heaps of goodies lying in our courtyard. It was a daunting task even for them to think what to do with all that perishable stuff! Certainly they would take some with them to their house – but the rest?

In those days we did not have a refrigerator in our house; nor did any of our friends or relatives. It was a good fifteen or twenty years later that people started having refrigerators in their homes. Having no means of storing all the sweetmeats, the best we all could think of was to distribute them to our wider family and to the neighbours who were already devouring the things with their greedy eyes.

It was quite a job to decide how much and what to send to which households, and it had to be done in as short a period as possible, or the things would start rotting. Soon they would be smelly and stale; in two or three days the rats and the ants would get to them and then they would be no good to anyone. Jiji helped us to make packages for distribution to our friends and neighbours, and our Servants got busy delivering them to the different households. The servants themselves feasted for several days on end.

Some days later when we phoned our oldest sister who lived in Jaipur to tell her about these farewell gifts she immediately said, "Why did you not send some for me and my family here in Jaipur?"

Oh yes, that was a blunder on our part. We should have thought about it. Our young brains could not think that far off in those days. It was too late by then. Most of the things had already been disposed of.

It was a nice feeling for us children that our father was so much loved and respected by his office staff. It was very considerate of them to think of saying their farewell to our father in this way. The gifts were ephemeral – of no lasting value or importance – but what was important and of lasting value were the combined good wishes and blessings from so many people at the same time. I feel sure that all those sincere wishes conveyed from their hearts went a very long way in my father's life and we children shared the good life and the good time with him for a long time after his retirement from the Central Government Service in Delhi.

Chand Jiji, our eldest sister at Jaipur, still remembered the incident when my brother read this story to her about two years before her death in 2008.

THE DIVINE BOUGH

"No, no, sir, we can't take the boat out today."

"Why?"

We children looked at the boatman as if it was very impertinent of him to say no to our request. We were just not used to hearing no from anyone working under my father.

"Why? Why won't you take the boat out?"

We had enquired with authority as if demanding him to do as he was told.

This is an incident of the bygone years when the maharajas still ruled over their states in India. In 1947, the Maharaja of Udaipur had invited my father to work for him as chief irrigation engineer. In those days a chief engineer's post was a highly privileged and prestigious position. My father was often invited by the Maharaja for formal dinners and consultations with him at the palace. We children, too, enjoyed all the respect and privileges given to officers' children. My younger brother was always addressed as 'Kunver Saheb' and we sisters were called 'Bai Sahibas' – respectful words for girls and boys – so we had got used to commanding respect from everyone around.

All the servants in those days were highly subservient and would not contradict or question anything that they were told to do. That is why hearing a no from a boatman was a bit unexpected. So we asked him again: "Why won't you take the boat out today?"

The boatman was an elderly, experienced person. Humbly he replied, "Jee Bai Sahiba, the weather is not right to take the boat out today."

This was the height of stupidity, we thought. It had been so hot and humid for the past four or five days that it was the most desirable and natural thing to do when we saw a boat standing idle by the lake.

We children – that is, our elder sister, our younger brother, younger sisters and I – often used to accompany our father when he went to the Jai Samand Lake for his official work during our summer holidays. The Jai Samand Lake is one of the biggest lakes in Rajasthan, about sixty kilometres south of Udaipur. Actually it is the second largest artificial lake in the whole of Asia, about fifty miles long; the width varies, according to the formation of the mountains around it, and it is said to be almost five miles deep in certain places. The Maharaja Jai Singh had the beautiful dam constructed in the seventeenth century at a place where the lake is comparatively narrow and shallow. The dam is about a furlong long and about thirty feet wide, with about twenty-five steps leading down to the lake shore. It is said that the lake is about 200 feet deep at the dam site.

Attached to the dam is the Maharaja's palace, built for the royal family to stay in whenever they went to the lake for picnics, boating, shooting excursions, etc. In those days all the hills around the dam and the palace were full of all kinds of dangerous wild animals, including lions, panthers, tigers, leopards, hyenas and, of course, plenty of snakes. The Maharaja often used to go to the Jai Samand Lake palace for a leisurely break and big-game hunting, which used to be a great sport of all the maharajas of that time.

Whenever we children happened to accompany our father to the Jai Samand Lake, a part of the palace was opened for us to stay in, with a retinue of servants to wait on us. That summer of 1948 our older sister, Radhe Jiji, Jijaji and their children, were visiting us from Delhi. My oldest sister's children had also come from Jaipur during their summer vacations and with them their first cousins had also come. In addition, the children of my father's colleague Mr Puri, who were our ages, were also there. In all we were quite a large party of children who had gone to the Jai Samand Lake for a two or three day excursion.

On the first day after breakfast we children were strolling on the dam when we spotted a boat moored at the corner of the dam. Normally there were no boats there. In those days, not many tourists went so far just for boating or sightseeing. However, we had heard from the locals that the Maharaja had his own private boathouse where his big steamboat and a few small rowing boats to accompany the royal boat were moored for the rare festive occasions when the Maharaja ventured out on the lake. We had never seen the royal boat or any other boat out on the open lake except on one occasion, when we had accompanied our father on his inspection tour. Nor had we seen any other people there, except those who were connected with the palace in one way or another. The only people we used to see around were the people who served the Maharaja, or the government officials and their staff.

That day there was a boat there, and when we saw it we could not resist the temptation of going out boating. The boatman was summoned. He came but hesitated to take us out. The matter was taken to the higher authorities. My father was very busy with his official work, but some other officers came out.

On their asking the boatman, he humbly said, "Sir, it has been so close for the past four or five days that not a leaf has stirred, not a whiff of a wind has blown, that a storm is imminent now and could strike any time. Taking the boat out would be a bit too risky and could be dangerous."

The officers saw the sense of what the boatman was saying and looked at us. To us brothers and sisters it did not matter. We used to go to Jai Samand Lake so often that it did not matter at all if we went boating that day or not, but the rest of the children who had come to Udaipur for the very first time did not want to miss this rare opportunity of going out boating on one of the most famous lakes in Udaipur on such a hot day. Our father's friend's children were the most enthusiastic of all. The lake and its water were just too tempting for all of us.

Most boisterous youngsters, if they are in a jubilant mood, cannot understand the perils connected with taking chances with water and other forces of nature, however much the elders and experienced people may tell them not to do so. If they want a thing they simply must have it. No dissuading will prevail.

When all the children persisted, the officer asked the boatman, if the storm had not struck so far why did he think that it would strike in the next few minutes.

"It may not hit for another day or two. Surely nothing is going to happen in the next few hours!"

So they told the boatman to take us for a very short, ten-minute round trip along the coast, keeping the boat close to the mountains, and turn back from the point where the opposite mountains protrude into the lake, leaving a very narrow strait to the main lake. In this way, even if a storm struck, it wouldn't hit the boat hard. The poor boatman had no say after that. Willy-nilly he brought the boat near to the steps and we children boarded the boat triumphantly. I remember for sure that it was just us children, with no other adult man except the boatman with us.

Our Jijaji had preferred to stay behind, looking after his small sons. My brother by nature is not a great lover of water, and after a narrow escape in a school boating excursion he was not at all interested in going out boating again, so he had stayed behind with Jijaji and our small nephews. The only male members in the group were my father's colleague's two young sons, who were about twelve and fourteen years old. My sister, Radhe Jiji, was the eldest person on the boat. She too would have gladly stayed behind with her husband and children, but being the eldest amongst us, she thought it would not be right to leave the irresponsible youngsters, especially with the guest children as well, to go out on their own in the boat. So as a duty towards the youngsters she boarded the boat as a guardian. In all we were about six or seven girls and two boys in the boat.

The ride started leisurely, everyone enjoying themselves to the full, laughing, chatting and joking. We would have loved to put our hands in the lake and have fun playing with the water just a few inches below the boat's sides; but we had been warned not to do so because there were plenty of crocodiles of all sizes in the lake, so we resisted the temptation.

The boatman rowed very cautiously. He had planned to take us on a circular route, rowing along the mountains on the right side and returning back by the left side along the opposite mountain range. From the dam, one doesn't get a full idea of the vastness of the lake, which stretches to its full width only beyond the nearby strait. I had seen that vast vista of water on an earlier boat trip. The topography of the lake is such that from the dam it looks like a small lake surrounded by mountains on all sides, but actually it is not so. Only a short distance from the dam, two opposite mountains slope down into the lake, leaving only a narrow strait leading to the vast lake beyond.

The ride up to that point was extremely pleasant, but no sooner had the boatman turned to the left to cross the narrow strait when suddenly *'Shoon! Shai! Gharrad, Gharrad!'*, thunder and bolt, the vicious storm hit us with full force, throwing the unwary of us out of our seats to the floor of the boat. The boat was swept along like a straw and was becoming totally uncontrollable. It shook with every gust of wind. The boatman was having a hard time in trying to keep it steady. With great skill and hard work he had managed to keep his grasp on the oars and crossed the narrow gap, but the force of the wind was so strong that the boat was automatically thrown towards the mountain's edge on the other side. The youngest of the children started shrieking and crying. Even we the older ones were shivering with sheer fright. It looked as though the boat would overturn at any moment in the mighty gales. It was only the skill of the boatman that saved the boat from turning over and crashing against the mountains. We could see how hard he was trying to keep the boat steady and, at the same time, at a safe distance from the mountain.

But wait! What was happening? Why had the boat started tilting? It did not take long for the boatman to realise what was happening. The water was deeper at that place than at any other spot on that small part of the lake. We were drifting towards the most perilous place on the lake. The boatman's worst fear had been realised. We were drifting towards a whirlpool.

We children did not have the faintest idea that there were whirlpools in the lake so near the dam and so near the mountains, and perhaps the boatman also did not expect a whirlpool in that little part of the lake. Once the realisation dawned on him, he felt the floor of the boat slipping under his feet. He let go of the oars and jumped from the lower end of the boat to the raised end to maintain its balance. We children were already in a state of panic trying hard not to cry. All our chatting and singing had long vanished with the wind. We just hoped and prayed that we would reach the shore safely – but where was the safety?

Suddenly we realised the boat was not only tilting, but also going round and round in circles. Unawares we were caught in a whirlpool. What were we to do now?

A whirlpool is like a gigantic bowl and the centre is much lower than the sides. If one gets caught within its pull, there is normally no escape!

It was no longer possible for the boatman to keep control over the boat. One end of the boat was being dragged down towards the centre of the whirlpool and the other stood almost at forty-five degrees. We children had to hold on tight to the wooden boards on which we were sitting to stop ourselves falling into the water. The boatman had to jump from the lower end of the boat to the raised end continuously to keep it steady and to stop it from capsizing.

Below was the whirlpool and above thunder and lightning. Added to the wild waves and high winds, the rain started pouring down cats and dogs. We were all at our wits' end. It was the most hair-raising moment of my life and of the others on the boat as well, I think. Was this going to be the end of us? Were we all destined for a watery grave?

No, God, No!

The boatman kept on jumping from one side of the boat to the other trying to keep its balance and at the same time trying to keep it away from the centre of the whirlpool. Unfortunately that was all that he could do; he could not control the boat any longer. Having no hope left, in sheer desperation he asked us to chant God's name, saying, *"Ram, Ram boliye bai sahib, Ram, Ram boliye."*

Crying for our lives we all started calling God aloud: "Ram, Ram, Ram, Ram."

The boatman's strength was slipping away. Exhausted though he was, he kept on leaping from one side of the boat to the other trying to keep it from being dragged down by the whirlpool and capsizing.

The lake, which was so calm and attractive a while ago, had suddenly turned into a devilish, dark death bowl. The waves were leaping, rough and high, ready to devour us any time. Our hopes of survival were fading away fast, and the heavy downpour of squally rain was now beginning to fill the floor of the boat. The boatman was at his wits' end and so were we all. Radhe Jiji alone kept her composure and continued chanting God's name with utmost sincerity. We were all trying our best to follow her example.

Desperate and helpless, fearful of a watery grave, we all started calling God even louder, with one voice: "Ram, Ram, Ram, Ram."

Then, lo! and behold! What happened? The boat stopped going round and round as suddenly as it had started. It looked as though our prayers had been heard. Our screams had reached God!

The boat not only stopped going round and round in circles but also became steadier. How did it happen? What miracle was this? We looked at the boatman, and to our great surprise we saw him holding tight with both his hands to a thick, brown bough of a big tree, keeping his feet firmly stuck on the boards of the boat. Where from had that bough suddenly appeared – that too exactly above our boat, where it was easily within reach of the boatman's hands as he was jumping from one side of the boat to the other? There is a saying that to a drowning man a frail blade of grass is enough support (*'Doobte ko tinke ka sahara'*). To me it looked as though God Himself had extended His own hand to draw us out of our ordeal. How else was it possible for a bough from a tree high up on the mountain to bend down so much as to come within reach of the boatman's hands? It was nothing short of a miracle. Without divine intervention the boatman would surely have found himself hanging in the air, holding on to the branch. But no, he held tightly to the strong bough, but kept his feet firmly stuck on the boards of the boat. Perhaps a sudden gust of wind had bent a big tree over the lake without uprooting it, with one single sturdy bough extending over the centre of the boat. To us at that time it was difficult to understand its appearance. We only knew that by holding on to it the boatman had somehow managed to stabilise the boat. It was nothing short of a miracle. It looked as if God Himself had extended His own helping hand to save us from our ordeal.

The boatman, holding tightly on to the bough, using his feet alone, managed to steady the boat and forced it out of the grip of the whirlpool. As he brought the boat closer to the mountain's edge, miraculously the storm seemed to drift away from us. We were no longer entirely at the mercy of the merciless wind.

Once out of the vicious grasp of the whirlpool, the boatman took back his oars and steadied the boat and thanked God in his own way. We could clearly see how relieved he looked, but he was completely exhausted – unable even to row the boat. But, what could we do? None of us knew how to row. None of us knew how to swim. Even if we had shouted for help, who could have heard?

Now that we were out of our ordeal, our nerves steadied a bit. The sky also cleared a bit and we realised that we were not at all far from the dam, where people were standing, braving the rain and wind, worrying about us and wondering what could they do to help us? There was perhaps nothing much that they could do, but they were trying all the possibilities they could think of to help us. Some of them were desperately trying to summon the driver of the Maharaja's steamboat to rescue us. Others were trying to find a big rope to throw at the boat. If the boatman had been able to tie it to the boat, then they could have drawn the boat towards the dam. Nobody could muster the courage to jump into the rough water of the lake – it was too dangerous to swim even in calm water because of the crocodiles. In rough water it was doubly dangerous. My father's eyes were fixed on the boat, as he prayed for the safety of all of us children.

However, what more help did we need, when God Himself had come to our rescue! The boatman somehow managed to row the boat cautiously to the dam's edge, but the lake was still very rough with high waves. Many people who were standing on the dam came down the steps and some of them, with the help of bamboo boathooks, managed to bring the boat up to the lake shore by the steps. Then they helped us climb down one by one from the boat. The younger children had to be carried in their laps. We, the older ones, still dizzy with fright managed to climb up the steps with our shaky feet.

Oh God! What a relief it was to be on the solid, even ground of the dam again! We and every one at the dam thanked God from the bottom of our hearts. It was only by His grace that our lives had been saved that day. Had He not extended His hand in the form of that bough, who knows what would have happened!

To this day I feel grateful to Him for His great mercy on us all. He alone saved us from the jaws of death on that frightful, stormy day.

So many years have passed by – so much water has flowed under the bridge – yet the incident is as fresh in the memories of all those who were there in the boat on that stormy day as if it had happened yesterday (as I verified on telephone talks before I started to write this account of our miraculous escape).

Had the Divine hand in the form of that bough not come over our boat I would not have been here to tell you this story today!

We learnt two very precious lessons a very hard way on that fateful day: never ever disregard the advice and experience of your elders, and never take chances with the forces of nature.

YOU WOULD NOT BELIEVE IT

You would not believe it, but it is as true as your own existence at this time holding this book in your hands and reading it. This is an account of an incident which was witnessed and shared by my children, my husband, my nephew and a student of my husband. It had happened in the bygone years of the sixties. I was about thirty-four years old and had a young family. My eldest son was just about eleven, my younger son about nine and my daughter about seven years old. We had returned from America and I was about three months pregnant.

Since 1955, I had started having migraine headaches. They used to start sometime in the middle of the night and by morning I would be in a terrible state. The headaches used to be so bad that even if I moved my head by a fraction of an inch I would throw out whatever I had eaten the night before. When my stomach was empty, some slimy, whitish liquid would come out and churn my stomach inside out and my head felt like bursting apart in pieces with throbbing pain as if someone was pounding it with a heavy hammer – 'dhonk, dhonk, dhonk!' I could neither sit nor speak. I used to be in indescribable agony. The painful condition used to last for at least twenty-five to thirty hours. I just had to lie down all bundled up with my eyes closed. To keep them open was a great effort and very stressful. I really can't describe how awful I used to feel. Only those who suffer from this kind of migraine can understand the feeling. All types of medicines were tried from allopathic to homeopathic to Ayurvedic to Granny's home-made remedies to charms and mantras, etc.

My own oldest brother is a doctor. He tried every possible medicine he could think of, but nothing worked. On one occasion an elderly lady who was visiting us made three small cup-sized wells of cow dung, filled them with water and I was asked to peep into them and recite a magic mantra. This was extremely, extremely difficult for me because, as I have already mentioned, I just could not move my head even by half an inch without vomiting. Getting up and reciting the mantra was out of question, because as soon as I tried to sit and open my mouth, vomiting would start, with turmoils in the tummy and hammering in the head.

Then in 1960 I went to America with my three little children to join my husband, who was already there since 1959. There our American doctor friends tried the latest medicines, which, even if they did not completely cure me, were supposed to ease the pain. I don't know how much they really helped me, because in October 1961, when we came back to India, the migraines were still bothering me.

In August 1962 my nephew, Chobi, from Jaipur came to visit us in Pune. He wanted to see the National Defence Academy at Khadakwasla, not far from Pune, before deciding his future career. It was not at all difficult for us to take him there because the principal of the academy, Mr Varma, was our family friend. We were sure that not only he would be happy to show Chobi around the academy, but also he would be happy if we had lunch with him. That is what he normally liked us to do whenever we went to Khadakwasla, but my nephew, being a shy young lad, did not want to meet the principal nor have lunch with him at this stage. In that case we thought it was best that only my husband would take my nephew to the academy and I would stay at home and keep the lunch ready for them on their return.

Now, as it happened, the day they decided to go, which was a Sunday, my migraine started – fortunately not in the middle of the night as it usually did but in the early hours of the morning. It had not yet reached the intensity of the migraines which started in the middle of the night, so I thought I should quickly put the main dish (*Karhi*) to cook before the migraine flared up in its full intensity. I got up, went to the kitchen and started the preparation.

Karhi is a favourite delicacy of the Mathurs. Enjoyed by old and young alike, it is made with yoghurt and gram flour, but it is a little bit tricky to make. So I thought it best if I could make it before the headache got too bad. Our servant boy did not know how to make it, so I decided to make it myself and allow it to cook on a slow fire for a few hours. It tastes best when cooked on a slow fire for three to four hours. The rest of the food I knew my husband (with some help from our servant) would manage to prepare.

No sooner I had heated the oil, added the spices and poured the mixture of yoghurt and gram flour into the hot pan on the stove, my head started reeling. I had to rush out of the kitchen and run to the sink and had a big vomit. Then I hurried to my bedroom and threw myself onto the bed, doubled up with a splitting headache. I could neither speak nor sit because it made me vomit again. I just lay down and closed my eyes, but my terrible headache would not let me lie down quietly. Again and again I was sick and threw up the slimy liquid. The fumes of the spices had made my migraine worse than ever before.

It was a very hot August summer day. My husband felt that if I kept on vomiting like that, I would get totally dehydrated. He tried to make me drink some water but, even a drop of water was impossible to take as it would immediately come out, making my condition worse.

Seeing me in that condition, my husband, Professor Mathur, decided that he would not go to Khadakwasla with my nephew; instead he arranged for a student of his to accompany my nephew to the military academy. It took some time to make this arrangement and it was nearing 11 a.m. when they left.

Our servant boy had made breakfast for them and lunch for our children and our guest, and by 1.30 he had fed the children, tidied up the kitchen and left for his home, which was very near our house. He often used to go back to his house in the afternoons unless there was some urgent work at our place. Since our guests had left late it was not expected that they would return before 3 or 4 p.m. By car it would have been quicker, but we had no car in those days. They decided to go by autorickshaw, which was faster than the bus, but for the return journey they would have to take a bus because there were no autorickshaws available at the academy in those days.

My husband himself had no lunch, saying that he would eat with our guests on their return, but he kept on asking me after short intervals if I had any inclination to have anything at all. In the beginning I kept on saying, "No, no, no," but at about 2.30 p.m. I felt that I could perhaps lick some ice.

In those days we did not have a fridge in our house – we had bought a very big one in America, but it had not yet arrived – so there was no ice in the house. Our servant boy was also not there. My husband did not want to go out leaving me alone in that condition. The heat was at its height at that time and the nearest shops from our home were almost a mile away, so I myself did not want him to go out in that scorching heat, walking all the way (we had not bought a car till then). My condition was getting worse and worse and my husband was getting more and more concerned, especially as I was pregnant. He wanted me to have a few drops of water at least, but I was not able to retain even a drop of water. Somehow, as stated earlier, I felt that perhaps I could lick some ice but unfortunately there was no way we could get some. How I wished our fridge had arrived! Also, our servant boy was not there to get it from the market. As the minutes ticked by, the headache grew worse and worse. The pounding and throbbing increased with each tick; and my throat became more and more parched, increasing my craving for ice. God, if only there was some ice!

Suddenly we heard the sound of thunder and lighting and big drops of rain started pouring down. August is a month of monsoons in India, so there was nothing unusual in that. What was unusual was the thick downpour of big hail stones. Our children rushed in, shouting, "Dada, Dada, come out and see the big hailstones. Look how big they are!"

I could not open my eyes, but I could hear what they were saying. It was absolutely unbelievable. Hailstones in that heat? Impossible!

We do sometimes have hailstorms in the winter rains in December and January, but rarely in summer – but there they were. The children insisting on dragging their daddy out into the back courtyard to see the big hail stones pouring down from the blue sky above.

My husband was absolutely astonished at the sight. Quickly he ordered the children to rush to the kitchen and get some big pots and pans to collect the hailstones. He himself fetched the biggest brass platter with raised high edges (*paraat*), which is usually used to prepare the dough for the chapattis. By the time they all went to the kitchen and brought out pots and pans, the hailstones had completely covered the whole back yard. They wanted to collect as many as they could, but the size of the hailstones raining down discouraged them from going out as they hit hard on their heads.

Suddenly the hailing stopped as suddenly as it had started, leaving a thick layer of hailstones all over the back yard.

My children and my husband picked up as many as they could and brought them in to show me. With difficulty I managed to open my eyes and was dumbfounded at the sight! So many hailstones and so big – almost the size of ping-pong balls! And on such a hot summer day! So much ice! Just the thing I wanted so badly!

My husband said happily, "Look, you wanted some ice – God has sent it for you."

My eyes were already wide open in sheer astonishment. I could not believe my eyes. Such big hailstones at the height of summer and in such abundance! It was absolutely unbelievable, but there they were right in front of me. My husband took one in his hand and touched it to my lips. There was now no question of believing or not believing!

The licking of the ice had a very soothing effect on me and a sort of peace descended on my body. I think I actually I slept for about half an hour or so.

On getting up I felt much lighter and clearer in my head. The head was still heavy but the pounding and throbbing had gone.

My first thoughts on getting up were for my nephew, Chobi, and my husband's student, Mr Sobhag Narayan. They had gone by autorickshaw but were to return by bus. I hoped and prayed that they had not been struck by lightning, had not been hurt by the big hailstones falling on their bare heads, and had not got wet in the rain on their way back on foot to our home from the bus stop. The size of the hailstones was big enough to hurt any body out there on the road.

In a little while I saw them coming in, all dry, chatting and laughing.

"Thank God!" I said to myself.

To my great astonishment, after sucking a part of a big hailstone I could now actually sit up and say a full sentence without vomiting!

I asked, "Are you OK? I hope you did not get wet and were not hit by the heavy hailstones."

They both looked at me in utter amazement: "What rain? What hail? When? Where? We met no rain or hail anywhere on our way. It is absolutely dry everywhere." Perhaps they thought that my headache had turned me crazy and that was why I was talking of rain and hail in that scorching heat and brilliant sunshine.

Just then the children showed them the pots and pans full of the hailstones. They were as astonished as we were initially.

"Where did you get them from?" they asked in utter disbelief.

The children took them to our backyard. They were absolutely amazed and bewildered beyond belief to see the ground all white with big hailstones.

"How could that be?" they wondered.

It was totally unbelievable to them and very hard to understand. They took my husband, holding his hand, to the front of the house.

"Look! It is all dry – not a drop of rain or hail."

Wonders! My husband saw for himself that the front of the house, the steps, the garden and all around were absolutely dry in the brilliant sunshine. He could not believe his eyes! The front of the same house so dry and bright and the back so wet and white!

My children, my husband, my nephew and Mr Sobhag Narayan all went out of the house in sheer curiosity to see if it had rained or hailed elsewhere. They found absolutely no sign of any rain or hail anywhere else at all.

How did it happen? How had our backyard alone got such a heavy downpour of big hailstones? The soil was still wet and white with hailstones, which were melting away fast by now. It surely was a wonder of wonders! Totally unbelievable! How was it that it hailed so heavily in our backyard and nowhere else? There was no sign of hailstones in the front, or anywhere else nearby, except for a few hailstones that had rolled over across the sparsely planted hedge along the wire fence.

Hard to believe, but it did actually happen. I know it is not easy to believe such an unusual phenomenon. At that time we ourselves did not think much about it. We were much more excited than astonished.

Now as I write I feel as if my own mother was somewhere around and had rushed in to help an ailing child of hers. Since I had lost my worldly mother in childhood, it could only be the Divine Mother who had showered Her Divine Grace on me in the form of those heavenly hailstones. I was not only relieved from my migraine in just six or seven hours instead of thirty-forty hours, but since then I have never had that sort of headache ever again.

Out of season, under the scorching sun, those heavenly hailstones had *healed me completely for good* from the terrible migraine headaches I used to suffer from for the past seven/eight years. I have never ever again suffered from those terrible type of migraines ever since.

Isn't it hard to believe? Perhaps you still don't believe, but God's ways are strange – not easy to explain!